When I left the Trappist mon
mane in Kentucky, I developed simp
contemplative prayer communities t̲ ̲ ̲ ̲ ̲ ̲ ̲ ̲ ̲ ̲faithful to the spirit of
contemplative Christianity that I had experienced in the monastery.
Donna has expanded these guidelines and added insights to make
this a valuable resource for groups and individuals where sincere
seekers can deepen their experience of God's presence in their lives.

James Finley, Ph.D
Renowned retreat master, Merton scholar,
and author *Merton's Palace of Nowhere* (25th anniversary edition)

This is a magnificent work! It is an excellent introduction to
contemplative prayer.

Dr. Pat Mitchell, professor emeritus St. John's Seminary.

Scientific research has generated evidence showing the healing
benefits associated with meditation. Conceived out of over 20 years
of facilitating contemplative groups, this book will teach you ways
to begin, develop and sustain a contemplative practice by finding a
focus for spiritual thought and openness to God, and for examining
your consciousness to more deeply understand what's driving your
thoughts and behaviors. *The Ground of God* is a precious legacy we
will treasure always.

Pamela Davidson, PhD, UCLA Research Scientist

The Ground of God is a gift for every soul desiring deeper
relationships with God and one another. Donna has a profound
gift of teaching and written expression. Strikingly simple in conception and format, this book provides guidelines for groups and
individuals to develop a disciplined rhythm of reading, praying
and examination. With the distractions and tensions of the world
today, it is timely for all of us to turn to our ancient and sacred
roots grounded in contemplation.

Michelle Waters, author *The Orange Line: A Woman's Guide
to Integrating Career, Family and Life*

About Donna Marie Ennis

Donna is from Seattle, Washington and has lived for many years in Manhattan Beach, California. She and her husband have raised three children and now have eight grandchildren. These family members are Lutheran, Catholic and Jewish. She says, "I have very generously been provided with the vision I feel is essential for our progress. I have come to see from the contemplative perspective we do not see the boxes, limits and divisions that can be drawn by some according to faith lines. Together we share the potential to see more deeply into the common truth that is central to our existence: each one of us is loved and called precious in God's sight." Donna has found that place of common ground in *The Ground of God*.

As a pianist Donna has spent a lifetime practicing rhythm, harmony and balance. As a spiritual director she has followed the lessons given by her teachers in music and in meditation and has been facilitating contemplative prayer groups and examination retreats since 1996. Donna has a broad base of insights gathered from a BA in Sociology and in completion of Spiritual Direction programs from Archdiocesan Institutes in Retreats and Spiritual Direction, Los Angeles (1990), as well as certification from the School for Charismatic Spiritual Directors, Pecos Benedictine Abbey in Pecos, New Mexico (1992), a six weeks in-residence program living the Benedictine way. Donna also draws insights from Myer-Briggs typologies and completed qualification with the Association for Psychological Type (APTi) in 1994.

While we can benefit from the courses we take,
and the work we do as well as the relationships we keep,
our spiritual enrichment is in remembering that
whenever I walk with another,
there is my teacher. – Donna

About *The Ground of God*

Remove the sandals from your feet, for the place on which
you are standing is holy ground. — Exodus 3:5

The Ground of God has four sections. All four sections are intended to work together to encourage a rhythmic cycle of read, pray and examine. The reader is drawn step by step into an active and wholly engaging spirituality, leading to the question: What on earth is so commanding? Who is in command? The title is taken from Exodus 3:5 "Take the sandals from your feet, for the place where you stand is holy ground." The reader is reminded that the holy ground is the ground where we stand, and the nature of contemplative prayer is closer than my hand is to my face.

The most unique feature of *The Ground of God* is its appeal to the contemporary reader. The outwardly active contemporary reader may feel disinclined to pick up and read a whole book on contemplation, mysticism and the church. *The Ground of God* covers the essence of all three facets of our faith life, presented in short sections easily accessed in any order. The inspired reader can flip anywhere; any page within each section stands alone with brevity and completeness of thought. When the reader can step back, it can be seen that each piece works with the next to complete the whole. The reader can begin to see more clearly the unfettered truth that is central to our existence: I am loved and called precious in God's sight.

For one who is new to contemplation, ease and simplicity of thought gradually open one up to the experiential knowledge that living a balanced life is within reach. For one who has contemplative prayer experience, the ancient, stable and holy ground of contemplative prayer is known with affirming clarity, depth and simplicity in new ways. The reader can begin to wonder: the Israelites had already wandered in the desert for 40 years in search of the Promised Land. Do I need to wait so long?

Remove the sandals from your feet, for the place on which you are standing is holy ground.
– Exodus 3:5

The Ground of God

Contemplative Prayer for the Contemporary Spirit

Donna Marie Ennis

Energion Publications
Gonzalez, FL
2016

Msgr Cox,
(You) are a jewel
in the ground of God
and a rare treasure
to many. Donna

Epiphany 2017

All scripture quotations are from the New Revised Standard Version of the Bible (NRSV), copyright © 1989 by the Division of the Christian Education of the National Council of the Churches of Christ in the USA.

Cover photo: "The Poplar Grove,"
St. Andrew's Benedictine Abbey, Valyermo, California
Photographer: Donna Marie Ennis

ISBN10: 1-63199-299-6
ISBN13: 978-1-63199-299-5
Library of Congress Control Number: 2016958053

Energion Publications
P. O. Box 841
Gonzalez, FL 32560

energion.com
pubs@energion.com

This work is dedicated to the monks of
St. Andrews Benedictine Abbey, Valyermo, California
and to small groups everywhere who share
the unbroken bond of silence,
especially the contemplative prayer group
at American Martyrs Catholic Church.
These persons inspire me every day with their faithfulness.

Acknowledgements

Above all, thank you to my husband Donn, our two daughters and son, their spouses, and eight grandchildren who teach me every day what it means to be rich; and to Lyn and Bruce who loved us all so well.

Thank you also to David Grudoski who pointed the way; to Pastor David Brostrom who handed me an empty notebook; to Fr. Paul Siebenand who asked me if I'd ever read the autobiography of St. Therese of Lisieux; to Fr. Randy Roche, S.J. through whom I was given a timely spark of inspiration; to all my piano teachers who have taught me that I am a beginner, always beginning; to James Finley for teaching faithfulness to practice; to Msgr. John Barry and Deacon Fred Rose for the blessings of spirituality generosity; to faithful friends and spirited readers: Dr. Pat Mitchell, Laurie Oester, PhD, and Phyllis Nugent; to Sr. Jeanne Fallon, C.S.J. who pulled a book from her shelf and asked me if I'd ever thought of Energion Publications; and to Henry and Jody Neufeld at Energion Publications for bringing all points and pathways to one in *The Ground of God*.

TABLE OF CONTENTS

INTRODUCTION

Culturally and spiritually speaking our greatest needs today after food and shelter are for spiritual balance and belonging. I do not know this to be scientifically proven. I do know that in my personal journey, and in my encounters with others as a spiritual director, this is most certainly true.

Our families are active, our work is demanding and even in leisure we search in vain for a quiet café for conversation. We feel scattered in various directions. We can begin to feel like we are living life in fragments. There is in each of us a sacred knowing of what is too much and what is enough; it's a voice that merits listening. When we become still and attentive we can begin to build the ground of our prayer, the ground of our inmost sense of being, to be stronger than any of the external influences.

As a classical pianist I have spent a lifetime studying perfect balance, harmony and rhythm, learning and practicing the lessons that transfer over to all of life. As a spiritual director I have continued following the lessons given by my teachers in music and in meditation. What follows has been written for the contemplative prayer group at American Martyrs Catholic Church, Manhattan Beach, California where I have facilitated, and we have met weekly since 1996. Each week we begin again as a group to start simple and stay simple. In the silence of our prayer, we become aware that contemplative spirituality is so much more than a thin stream of consciousness reserved for a select few. Along the way we discover the pathway to a wholly engaging, full-bodied spirituality, grounded in the living word of God spoken today in the heart of the one who will pause to listen. Those who remain find what they are seeking: balance and belonging in the Body of Christ.

Overview

The Ground of God has four sections. All four sections are intended to work together to encourage the reader to develop a rhythmic cycle of read, pray, and examine. The material is presented using common sense, non-scholarly language easily understood by anyone at any level. For one who is new to contemplation, ease and simplicity of thought gradually open one up to the experiential knowledge that living a balanced life is within reach. For one who has contemplative prayer experience the ancient, stable and holy ground of contemplative prayer becomes known with affirming clarity, depth and simplicity in new ways. Living a prayer filled, scripture based life leads the reader to ask the question: What on earth is so commanding? Who is in command?

"Section One: The Ground of Our Prayer" defines the nature of contemplative prayer and its relevance to the outwardly active contemporary spirit: I am neither ahead nor behind; I am where I can be. The ground of our prayer by its very nature has a way of re-establishing our proper place in the kingdom of God. There is an order, balance and harmony created by God and all we have to do is listen for what our part is in it, often by taking time apart and separating ourselves from our outer life for a moment. Moses took off his shoes to stand on the ground that is holy. The holy ground remains and is ours today in order that we might remove our shoes and release our hearts to come before God empty handed and open hearted, trusting in God to bring us away from confusion, toward clarity of mind and heart.

"Section Two: Brief Spiritual Essays" provides short spiritual essays. The essays are grouped in six sets; each single essay stands alone with completeness and brevity of thought. The essays can be read in any order, singularly at random, or in the sequence of the set. The essays form a focus for spiritual thought and orient the reader toward openness to God in prayer. One essay is suitable for one period of contemplative prayer. Less is best; empty is better than full. The people of Israel were strongest when they had nothing else to rely on except the word of God.

"Section Three: Examination of Consciousness" offers unique and specific guidelines for individual examination of one's life awareness following basic themes of gratitude, examine, humility, forgiveness and commitment. Because the spiritual life is one of continual change the contemporary spirit is invited, even compelled to live a life in perpetual examination of one's thoughts and actions. The exercises offer a practical way to apply insights gained in reading and in prayer. The exercises are repeatable at any point in the spiritual journey.

"Section Four: Group Formation Guidelines" provides practical support for parish faith formation programs. The guidelines are also useful for establishing a disciplined, independent program for use at home in one's own time. While one can read through any of the guidelines given for the practice of contemplative prayer, being able to pray with a group on a regular basis is the better-known source of encouragement for one's individual spiritual development.

The most unique feature of *The Ground of God* is its appeal to the contemporary reader. The outwardly active contemporary reader is disinclined to pick up and read a whole book on contemplation, mysticism and the church. *The Ground of God* covers the essence of all three facets of our faith life presented in short sections easily accessed in any order. The inspired reader can flip anywhere; any page within each section stands alone with brevity and completeness of thought. When the reader can step back it can be seen that each piece works with the next to complete the whole. The reader can begin to see more clearly the unfettered truth that is central to our existence: I am loved and called precious in God's sight.

Along the way it becomes apparent: there is so much more to life than the obvious and living a balanced life is within reach. Through faithfulness in prayer we grow the ground within to be stronger than any other. We are seeing some surface tensions in the body of the church and in all of our human systems; in truth our mystical roots remain deep and strong, and silently they are so beautiful. They stand to serve us well today. There is much more to be said about them. This is the way of contemplation.

Section One: The Ground of Our Prayer

Remove the sandals from your feet,
for the place on which you are standing is holy ground.
— *Exodus 3:5*

THE GROUND OF OUR PRAYER

A child has a particular way of seeing the wind moving over a field of grass, or the sunlight shimmering through the trees in a way that becomes enviable as we grow older and take on all that life has to give. The spiritual line of vision for a child can lead directly to an awareness of a lighter, quieter and more reflective side to life. Such moments of blessedness most often occur in a quiet place, and come from out of the positive side of spiritual emptiness. They very often correspond to nature and may extend just beyond the daydream into holy ground, the ground of Abraham, Moses, Elijah and Jesus. With this vision there may come a sense of nurture, consolation and oneness. One might call this the beginning of contemplative prayer.

The ground of our prayer by its very nature has a way of re-establishing our proper place in the kingdom. There is an order, balance and harmony created by God, and all we have to do is listen for what our part is in it often by taking time apart and separating ourselves from our outer life for a moment. Moses took off his shoes to stand on the ground that is holy. The holy ground remains and is ours today in order that we might remove our shoes and release our hearts to come before God empty handed and open hearted, trusting in God to bring us away from confusion and toward clarity of mind and heart.

Through all of history we have seen continual movement from desolation to consolation and back again and again and ultimately forward. Life carries deep grief and pain; life also brings very great consolation. Ours is a living faith passed on from generation to generation. The one who prays does not pray alone. When we pray we join in a steady stream of prayer that began more than 2000 years ago. With the world around us in a constant state of flux there is a special grace in knowing there is a place that is sacred and unchanging, a place where we can go to be renewed in the love that is ours by way of God's grace. From the beginning of time it has been known that God's love longs to touch us, heal us and make us whole and is doing so in this very moment.

Our belonging is rooted in the ground of Moses, and those who came after him, in the holy ground of God nurtured and nourished by way of prayer. Through the course of every day there are many things that take us sideways or backwards stretching the roots of our existence, and challenging our stability in surprisingly new ways. An organism cannot live too far from its roots. Putting down roots, knowing our roots, touching our roots benefits us as it does the tree. The roots serve to stabilize the tree giving it belonging in the ground. Our shared mystical roots in the ground of our prayer remain constant and stable, continuous through time; nevertheless we waver in our spirituality moving unpredictably from security to instability, and then back again to the bedrock of the ground of God

Jesus invites us to be like the children. While a child can feel at one in the presence of the wind and the sun, over the course of time and through the years things change as we gradually take on all that life has to give. It can feel as if the ground beneath our feet has changed, but it hasn't; we have changed by taking on an existence that feels lacking in clarity. When we can separate for a moment from all that life has brought us we can know that God remains here for us, in our forgetfulness of self. When we can realize the convergence of the daydream and prayer with the quiet blessedness God bestows on us all, then we can know what it means to be rich. When we are spiritually rich our perspective is changed.

Everything in the spiritual life is preparation for what is to come. If we were asked to go on alone we would fail. Through prayer we are granted the grace to touch the stable ground that is holy and sacred and has been so from the beginning of time. In retrospect, in later years such moments of blessedness as may have been known in childhood can be seen as signs of God's grace longing to touch us, heal us and make us whole, whether in the emptiness of our perceived aloneness or in the fullness of quietude.

In touching the holy ground of our prayer we begin to yield to God's mysterious purpose.

Through faith we believe there is strength greater than ours longing to bring us toward clarity and wholeness, toward holiness, and our response is our prayer-filled yes. To this God stands pleased.

Remove the sandals from your feet,
for the place on which you are standing is holy ground.
– Exodus 3:5

WHAT IS CONTEMPLATIVE PRAYER?

"For your Father in heaven knows all of your needs."
– Matthew 6:8

Everyone's prayer experience is unique. There is no good, better or best way to pray. Most of us feel inclined to pray in varieties of ways. Over time we tend to develop a preference for one way, but not to the exclusion of other ways of prayer. We stay grounded in the process of prayer rather than attached to outcomes.

Our Christian tradition has retained three major expressions of prayer: vocal, meditative and contemplative (*Catechism of the Catholic Church* N. 2699). In vocal prayer we are asking, telling or thanking God about something. Examples of vocal prayer include liturgical and intercessory prayer and other kinds of spoken and written prayers of the church, as well as one's own conversations with God. Meditative prayer focuses on something: an object, a word or phrase, or a particular person or situation. We give focused attention, perhaps engaging eyes, mind, heart and hands. In contrast, in contemplative prayer there is no thing (nothing) before God. We meet God in silent surrender, empty handed and open hearted trusting in the subtle and transforming presence of God who knows all of our needs even before we do.

In stillness of mind and body we create time in our life and space in our hearts in order to be present to God's transforming grace. We profess our openness to God's will trusting in the mystical fact that each one of us possesses enormous potential beyond our present experience. Just for now we let go of the concerns of our hearts: all the people, places and things of our active life insofar as we are able. We open our hearts to God trusting that perhaps it is so that God wants to get a word in edgewise into our very active lives. It is our experience of God's transforming grace that can then be reflected back to all of life.

Contemplative prayer is not just a way of praying associated with saints and mystics who lived in another century. Our shared mystical roots with them run deep and strong. When we pray we join in a steady stream of prayer that has been in place since before the time of Moses. In our early history the desert fathers gave new life and vitality to the whole church returning by way of prayer to the mystical roots of the Body of Christ. They became advocates of silence and solitude. They were going against the grain of the times. Our contemplative roots can be traced to them.

In generalities we can apply to our lives what we have learned from them: keep originality of thought, keep your thoughts faithful to your heart, and keep your heart grounded in God. In disturbance of thought, draw closer to God. Verify yourself in God and not through the eyes of others. Beyond all understanding, God is at work in you, changing your heart before you can change your mind. From this perspective the desert father or mother, the hermit, or the monk is countercultural and so are we when we make the choice to spend a few moments or an hour, or all of our days in silent surrender to our God who loves us through each new breath and with every beat of our heart.

Every life has creative potential beyond our present experience. We trust in God's providence. In humility and simplicity we accept the gifts of God's love and grace that come to us along the way, for our Father in heaven knows all of our needs before we do (Matthew 6:8). All is by God's design. All is grace.

How is the Contemporary Spirit Different From Any Other?

Every generation re-imagines and re-invents communication with increasing speed and efficiency. Every generation is astounded with its effectiveness. Communications have become increasingly simplified leading to complexities never before experienced. Our immediate situation, as well as our global one, can pass from integration to disintegration and then back again faster than we could have imagined even a decade ago.

The mystery of paradox brings us closer to the truth. The contemporary spirit lives with a global awareness that was heretofore unknown. New ideas and technologies are dispensed faster than they can be diffused and assimilated. Changes in the ways and means of communication cause cultural changes that are not always synchronized with individual understanding and integration, and we feel effectively compromised. We are shaped by the world in which we live, and the contemporary spirit can feel inclined to live a disordered life far from our original and intended course.

In all of our systems, both sacred and secular, we have instant and unfiltered access to our work and to one another. Just as quickly as I am connected, I can disconnect. If I no longer favor the way communication is going I can press quit or delete or exit, and feel immediately relieved for having done so. If I am dissatisfied with my work, my relationships, or my church I can delete that too. We can find ourselves wandering in a contemporary urban wilderness unable to spot what is missing, and all of our systems are characterized by ease of exit. In plain language, we live at a faster pace much ahead of the pace of cultural and individual integration and our lives feel out of balance.

The practice of contemplative prayer can be a way for the contemporary spirit to seek and sustain balance as the ground of our prayer gradually becomes infinitely deeper and more stable than any of the external influences. The pendulum of the clock, like our cultural pendulum, swings far and wide. The perfect balance of stability is found at the center-point. Just as with the pendulum of the clock, our point of balance can feel fleetingly brief as we envision our return to new external influences, demands and deadlines and yet the center-point of truth remains: God loves us all unspeakably much.

Gradually and through committed practice the foundations of the ground of our prayer become stronger than any of the external influences. This is our ongoing conversion to a better way. Out of the love God has for us we come to know there is strength in gentleness, and it is a charismatic kind of strength that sets a person apart from the tensions of life. Here in prayer is where we find our touchstone for stability, a stability that increases gradually over time. With the world around us in continual interpersonal and technological transitions, there is a special grace in knowing there is a place that is sacred and unchanging, a place where we may remain to be renewed in the love that is ours by way of grace. But do we seek it? Some are beginning to say: yes, we do.

O that today you would listen to his voice! – Psalm 95:7

Confessing My Powerlessness

"Into your hands I commend my spirit." – Luke 23:46

The subject of contemplation is being introduced and widely promoted in the medical, psychological and corporate worlds under the concept of mindfulness, and has long been embraced in 12 step spirituality, where confessing my powerlessness is the initial step one takes toward spiritual awakening and transformation. Those discovering the benefits of mindfulness in the secular world are seeking the same benefits at a deeper level within the sacred context, where we find the ancient roots to what is being uncovered. The benefits gained with the practice of contemplation are for the well being of the individual and all of our human systems, for the good of the whole.

In various times and ways each one of us has tapped into the disorderedness and the unmanageability of life. When we continue to take on all that life brings to us, we can all too easily fall to the belief that our lives are too busy and that time goes by too quickly. We fall victim to our false self and away from the truth: time never changes. The passage of time is the same now as it was for Moses. Time cannot be managed. What we can manage is what we put into the time we are given. What we put into the time we are given and what we receive from it makes the feeling different.

We can begin to wonder: what on earth is so commanding? Who is in command? Cultural stimuli seek to keep us filled to overflowing. When the inner self is given free reign to mirror the outer we live our lives based in external influences, leading us to live interruptive lives far from our original intended nature filled with grace. Restlessness becomes the exit point based on one's experience that life does not appear to be working in the given moment. I may feel confusion, as if I have lost my faith when indeed I have grown out of the faith that once was mine: God may be guiding me along the way of a deeper avenue of faith.

The paradox is that restlessness in relationships, in community, and in prayer may be a sign that a person is clearly on the brink of a deeper spirituality. If we are satisfied with our present condition, if we are comfortable with the present state of our soul or the state of the world, then we are not ready for the spiritual journey. I can take a step to correct the course of my interruptive life when I can delete some of the external voices, and when I can press pause for a moment to separate from what appears under false pretenses to be so commanding. The disciplined heart, which becomes the disciplined mind, has the capacity to turn inward returning to the stable base of our spiritual foundations, where peace and harmony are in command.

Restlessness, invitation and opportunity remain today, just as was so for Moses. We can be stretched by the tensions of conformity or we can find our ultimate rest, release and spiritual liberation in contemplation of our God who brings new life. Jesus shows us the way of peaceful release. The choice remains ours.

The pendulum of the clock swings far and wide finding the center-point of perfect balance at regular intervals. We can do no less than the clock. In contemplation, it's possible, for a moment in time, to find release from the fatigue of the tensions of effort and secular competition by confessing one's powerlessness and yielding to a strength that is greater than our own. We become quietly present in our open and undefended self to the presence of God. The transformative effects are to bring us back to our original and intended course, with a yearning for increased holiness and infinite goodness, in the company of a power greater than our own, longing to heal us and make us whole.

All of our systems are characterized by ease of exit, but God does not want us to be short changed. God pulled the Israelites out of the fray of life and spoke to them in the wilderness. Is this a time to pause and to seek our own spiritual wilderness? Is this a time to know in a deeper way the meaning of contemplation? Is this a time to find an hour of quiet, or to schedule a day or two of silence in a monastic retreat? Life has gaps. The Israelites had already wandered in the desert for 40 years in search of the Promised Land. Do I need to wait so long?

How Do I Begin?

I am interested in contemplative prayer; how do I begin? Jesus did not over-instruct. Contemplative prayer is the simplest expression of our faithfulness to the teachings of Jesus. When his disciples asked Jesus to teach them to pray, Jesus said: "Whenever you pray, go into your room and shut the door" (Matthew 6:6). Jesus went on to say don't use too many words (Matthew 6:7), and then he taught us to pray to our Father who is in heaven (Matthew 6:6-8).

Consistent with the teachings of Jesus, there are not too many instructions given for beginning a contemplative prayer practice. Ours is an incarnation theology. We believe that through Jesus, by the power of the Holy Spirit, God is within our hearts. Given the presence of God, we have everything we need within us, and through contemplation we become naturally present to God's grace. We stay faithful to the kernel of truth hidden away in *Catechism of the Catholic Church:* "Contemplative prayer is the simplest expression of the mystery of prayer" (N 2713).

In undefended openness we offer our silent surrender to our God who loves us here and now. It is as if we say: Lord I am here for you, and I know that you are here for me too. Every relationship is strengthened by clear and undefended openness, and this remains so with our God who loves us through every moment of every hour. We desire to be the empty canvas; God is the artist. If the canvas is kept still and quiet, the artist is quite inclined to achieve a most wondrous work.

Contemplative prayer is most often grounded in reading a passage from the sacred scriptures. Repeated readings are beneficial, as the words and actions of faith represented in the sacred texts can have an increasingly profound effect on our whole being. We are gradually transformed from the inside out. Over a period of time, we find that we are truly living the Word of God from our hearts out in to our active lives.

In the beginning, on one's own, it's better to be easy with the time frames and to eventually settle down into a pattern. Untrained human nature cannot sustain focused attention for one hour. For example if a wait in a doctor's office is for 10-15-20 minutes, it feels within the limits of our expectations. If a wait for anyone or anything goes over 25 or 30 minutes we begin to feel restless, annoyed and distracted. Most of us can manage 20 minutes. We stay within what feels manageable. However, if one begins with 5 minutes each day that may be 5 minutes more than was so yesterday.

To begin to pray set aside all that you carry with you in your heart and hands. Just for now set aside all the people, places and things of your active/outer life. Set aside also reading materials and other meditation objects. Take a moment to experience what it is like to entrust your whole sense of being completely to God. Prepare to receive God's presence and action within the holy ground of your being. We know that through Jesus, by the power of the Holy Spirit, God the Artistic Director of all souls is brought closer to us than our own thinking and even closer than touch.

Find a posture that gives you a balanced feeling in your body. Sitting with body weight balanced and with a straight back facilitates easier and deeper breathing. Breathing may become slowed as well as deeper as the outer things of life are released. We come to God empty handed and open hearted insofar as we are able, trusting that God knows all of our needs, and will care for us.

During prayer sounds come in from outside, and thoughts come up from within. Inner and outer distractions are a normal part of the prayer process. We do not eliminate thoughts from our mind; that would be an impossible task that would only take us sideways. We neither accept nor reject the thoughts that come. We merely acknowledge the interruptive nature of our restless mind. When the inevitable thoughts do come, it may be helpful to use a simple word or phrase to bring your focus back to God, that is, return to prayer. Your chosen word or words will be unique and special to you. Examples: "Jesus, have mercy," "Come Holy Spirit," "Lord, take me back" or "Change my heart, O God."

When contemplative prayer is practiced in a group setting, it is common practice to have a meditation walk between two periods of silent prayer. In the walking meditation we feel high regard for the space between us and the person behind and the person in front of us. The spaciousness between two or more is where the Holy Spirit lives and moves and breathes. The space is to be valued. The walking meditation is something we can practice metaphorically in every moment of every day. Every step we walk or every step we take in our thinking is either away or toward our completion and wholeness. Informed by God's grace, can I grow this spacious ground within to be deeper and stronger than any other that is known to me?

In my practice of contemplative prayer, questions I may ask: can I give myself the space that is needed in order for me to fully function in my life? Can I give the same to others? In the spaces between can I find the places of clarity in my life? By God's grace, can I grow the spiritual ground within my soul to be stronger than any other that is known to me?

While one can read through any of the guidelines given for the practice of contemplative prayer, being able to pray with a group on a regular basis is the better-known source of encouragement for individual prayer in one's own room. Most groups tend to offer two 20-minute periods of contemplative prayer within a one hour format. Regarding the practice and formation of contemplative prayer groups, further guidelines can be found in Section Four, "Small Group Formation Guidelines" (p. 117).

As we grow inwardly, and become more deeply grounded in our prayer, we also grow outwardly. In the faithfulness of our practice, we remain open to continual transformation and conversion to a better way. It is not particularly asking for anything more, but rather it is opening our heart to be changed by God's grace. We remain unattached to outcomes. If I am attached to outcomes, then I am attached to something that does not exist, and how can I be grounded in that?

In contemplation it becomes my deepest desire to let God speak into the empty places within my heart. Welcome the empty and open moments when they come. For prayer, empty is better than full. Trust in God's grace: God knows all of our needs. All is in God's hands. All is grace.

Be submissive as is the statue to the craftsman who molds it, to the artist who paints it, and to the gilder who embellishes it.
— St. John of the Cross, *The Minor Works*

Am I one who is called to pray in this way?

I will instruct you and teach you the way you should go.
— Psalm 32:8

Time will tell. Everybody brings something special, and each one of us has gifts differing. We all very naturally have our strengths and preferences. Our initial attraction to contemplative prayer is often temperament directed. Those whose lives are grounded in the interior functions of introversion and intuition may easily feel an affinity for contemplative prayer, and perhaps may naturally already be practicing contemplation. Those whose lives are more grounded in the external functions of thinking, sensing and action may acquire a brilliant balance in wholeness of temperament as the less preferred interior functions are brought to light. This is how one begins to know wholeness.

In the spiritual life nothing remains the same. The benefits of contemplation are made known gradually over time. God's grace does not get taken back. Because the graces of contemplative prayer come gradually, they tend to be cumulative and for keeps. True contemplative prayer will always be judged by how our lives are gradually changed. Change comes in the form of increased self-understanding and liberation from the confusion of common self-absorption to a fuller understanding of who I am within and beyond myself. Questions I may ask: 1) Because of my contemplative prayer practice am I gradually growing in God's love, peace and joy? 2) Is the growth I experience being reflected back to me in my relationships? 3) Through spiritual growth in my relationships am I being led to deeds of charity and mercy within and beyond my faith community?

God has given us a fairly level playing field. We are all more alike than we are different. We have individual needs that in some ways are the same as our collective needs for the stable, balancing force of God's love. Nothing draws us quite so powerfully as the love of God. Where I am loved, I will go.

Where there is no love, put love, and you will draw out love.
                                    – St. John of the Cross, *The Minor Works*

SOUNDS AND SILENCE, HARMONY AND BALANCE

"Peace I leave with you; my peace I give to you. I do not give to you as the world gives. Do not let your hearts be troubled, and do not let them be afraid." — John 14:27

"Lord, make me an instrument of your peace" is the first petition of the prayer of St. Francis of Assisi. An instrument is a means by which something is accomplished. An instrument is also capable of producing music, that is beauty, harmony and balance. Music is made up of notes and rests, sounds and silence. The rest is the space between notes, and tones are neither played nor sung into the rest. Contemplation is our rest between the notes of life. Where there is balance, harmony and rest, there is peace. Peace is our universal desire.

We experience life at two levels: the obvious and the sacred. There are times when the two become one, with the love of God leading the way to transformation and clarity of thought. For the saints and mystics of the church, this was so, often in the deepest pain of the struggles of life. Their stories convince us of the mystical fact of the possibility of the convergence of heavenly oneness with the imperfections of our earthly life: the two shall become one. Our restlessness along the way creates an inner tension between two points: our human will and God's will for us. The creative tension in the space between two points becomes the energy filled place where we are awakened to a larger dimension of life. This is the space where the Holy Spirit can live and move and breathe. This is the place where we begin to yield to God's transforming grace, the place of our ongoing conversion to Christ.

Jesus came to bear witness to all that is peaceful and good, the good that is the love of God. Jesus came to teach us the way we should go, the way of goodness. Those with whom Jesus walked were often outside the boundaries of goodness as determined by the establishment. In his teachings, no one is excluded for any reason we could witness or imagine. Jesus did not just come to teach goodness to the good; Jesus came to teach the one who would listen. Jesus kept company with the ones who would pause in their lives, to listen to him. Contemplative prayer is our time to pause in our life, to listen in silent surrender to the One who gives us life.

It is within the temporal emptiness of childlike surrender that space is created for the fullness of God's grace to enter in. Very often, it is in the empty spaces within us and in our relationships where the Holy Spirit is free to live and move and breathe. We remember that God's love longs to touch us and heal us and make us whole. We are reminded that somewhere along the way, we have become vessels of blessedness with the fullness of Christ. Why would I not say yes?

Christian renewal came from out of the desert and continues to come today in the hearts of all believers who are willing to expose the desert areas of the human heart to the living waters of the Love of God. At the close of the darkness of winter all of our hope is hinged on the solitary green leaf beginning to appear in the earliest part of the season of spring, bearing living proof that our strength is in our roots. We live life from this day forward.

For I am about to create new heavens and a new earth;
the former things shall not be remembered or come to mind.
                                                    – Isaiah 65:17

Section Two: Brief Spiritual Essays

I have loved you with an everlasting love. — Jeremiah 31:3

BRIEF SPIRITUAL ESSAYS

INTRODUCTION

The following essays were originally written for the contemplative prayer group at American Martyrs Catholic Church, Manhattan Beach, California where I have facilitated and we have met weekly since 1996. The essays expand on what is presented in "Section One: The Ground of Our Prayer."

The essays are grouped in sets; each essay stands alone with completeness and brevity of thought. They can be read in any order, singularly at random or in the sequence of the set. One essay is intended for one period of prayer. The reading forms a focus for spiritual thought and orients the reader toward openness to God in prayer.

In addition to a page or two of spiritual reading, contemplative prayer is most commonly grounded in reading a text from the sacred scriptures.[1] One may follow one's heart toward a chosen text or one may consult the daily lectionary of the church. Brief readings are suitable for contemplative prayer. Less is best; empty is better than full. The people of Israel were strongest when they had nothing else to rely on except the word of God.

At the close of prayer, it is common practice to pray The Lord's Prayer (Matthew 6:9-13). To begin the remainder of the day, take a moment to express your gratitude to God.

---

1   See "Reading the Sacred Scriptures: Lectio Divina" from Section Three on p. 102.

The Lord's Prayer
Matthew 6:9-13

1. *Our Father in heaven, hallowed be your name.*
2. *Your kingdom come*
3. *your will be done, on earth as it is in heaven*
4. *Give us this day our daily bread,*
5. *forgive us our debts, as we also have forgiven our debtors.*
6. *Do not bring us to the time of trial*
7. *rescue us from the evil one.*
8. The Doxology

> *The Lord's prayer is truly the summary of the*
> *whole gospel of Jesus.* – Tertullian

1. *"Our Father in heaven, hallowed be your name."*

Jesus teaches us to pray to our Father, naming us his brothers and sisters, daughters and sons of God united through all of life's trials and blessings. Jesus has called us into oneness with God in order to be with one another what is too difficult to be individually. Ours is an apostolic faith. Having one common Father, we transmit, that is we share with others what has become known to us.

We pray to our Father in heaven. Heaven does not refer to a specific place in time, but to God's unfailing grace that is continuous and everywhere and, through Jesus, by the power of the Holy Spirit is brought even closer to us than sight or touch. Heaven is the Father's house, the true homeland toward which we are heading and to which we already belong. We pray that God's unfailing love and grace will be with us in the same way on earth as it is in heaven. We learn with all these things to be at home, while still on the way with our Father who is holy in us and with us.

We meet God in complete surrender insofar as we are able. God's grace is made holy in us and comes to us with our open-hearted consent. We pray God's name may be kept holy in all of our thoughts, words and deeds. We pray that God's name be kept holy in others in whom, for lack of consent, God's grace still awaits. We feel protection is granted.

We pray that God's name be kept holy and sanctified in us, and that we may be granted the Spirit of cooperative grace to enter into God's master plan for all mankind. As we develop a closer relationship with God our capacity for grace and serenity grows with our years. Our vision of life becomes broader and extends beyond the obstacles of daily living. Our lives become less effort driven, sanctified by grace. We become guided by God through Jesus our brother, toward Love alone for the good of the whole, united as brothers and sisters with one common father.

2.   *"Your kingdom come,"*

The kingdom of God is the grace of God. It is impossible to put limits on God's grace. In our world and in the universe beyond God's grace is effective and very much at work. There is an order created by God; our role is to listen for what our part is in it. This is contemplation. We pray to be the empty canvass for God the Artist, the One who paints the sunrise and sunset in new ways every day.

God speaks to us through his Son by the power of the Holy Spirit, but this is not likely the loudest voice we will hear. Jesus often went to a quiet and deserted place to pray (Luke 5:16). We too seek moments apart in quiet prayer, to see more clearly into the order and balance and harmony that is already in place: this is God's kingdom come.

When we can know God's grace in the darkness of the challenges in our earthly life, then we can say: Lord I do believe your kingdom comes. St. John of the Cross says do not worry about any of your temporal goods such as riches, status, positions, dignity, or your children, parents or marriages (St. John of the Cross, *The Ascent of Mt. Carmel*, Ch. 18). Jesus says do not worry about your clothing, your food, or your tomorrow, for your heavenly Father knows all of your needs (Matthew 6:25-32). God meets us in our deepest need, and will grant us grace of the kingdom that is sufficient for today.

With all of the obstacles in the course of my daily life, if I can say that I am very gradually growing in the love, peace and joy of Christ, then I can say with my whole heart that I do believe "thy kingdom comes." Together we wait in faith for the complete, perpetual and universal fulfillment of this petition. This is the fullness of the kingdom we pray will come. When I can say with all of the obstacles to daily living that I have found some measure of peace, then for a moment in time I can say: God's kingdom comes.

3.   *"Your will be done, on earth as it is in heaven."*

Heaven is the perfection of God's majestic grace. Heaven is the place where the reconciliation of all things stands as mystical fact, and our invitation to be there is unceasing. Since we are of two natures in possession of a body from earth and a spirit from heaven, we are ourselves both earth and heaven, individually and collectively. We pray that God's will be done both in our body and in our spirit, as it is in heaven.

The will of God is above all a comprehensive plan for all of heaven and earth. By keeping a spirit of cooperation in my heart, I remain open to the love and the flow of God's perfect will in my life. Contemplative prayer is a way of very gradually correcting and purifying our desires. Contemplative prayer is our way of touching the stable ground of the love and truth that is God in our hearts.

We are called to make numerous decisions daily from the place where prayer and action meet. When a decision is made in accordance with God's will, I find that my faith is clearer and my efforts are less. Sometimes it seems that we are required to put together a very complex puzzle that we have been given, and it appears that some of the pieces are missing, but they aren't. God has given us all that is needed. We are invited to cooperate with God's spirit of grace as we wait to see the fullness of the vision God has for us.

Our lives are filled with many voices competing for our attention. We are each a person in process. We are called to a very special kind of listening, a listening with our hearts. Listening comes to us in the quiet with time set aside for personal prayer and reflection. God comes to us today to fill our hearts with wisdom and grace. It is our deepest desire to be facilitators of God's grace. For our imperfect following, for all of our resistance, for all of our doubts about our capabilities and responsibilities it is our heart's deepest desire to be good citizens of the kingdom.

4. *"Give us this day our daily bread."*

We pray to God to give us the daily bread that sustains us in our earthly life. Jesus teaches us to ask our Father for bread. In the language of God there is no I, me or mine. Everything is everyone's. There is one bread, one voice, and one body for us all. Bread is a necessity for us. Through the course of our day we continually use up our energy, eventually to death if this basic need is not met. This is the daily food we ask for. We know in faith and trust that God will give to us this day what is needed for today.

In order to receive our daily bread we need to not already be filled. If we are filled, we cannot take in. If we are filled with all the people, places and things of our outer life, our active life, then we cannot receive because there is no room.

> *For the Lord gives his blessing there, where he found the vessels empty.* – Thomas à Kempis, *The Imitation of Christ*

The bread of life we are given, the bread that sustains us, knows no bounds. The very bread we are given is the very bread we are asked to extend to another. We are all more alike than we are different. We have individual needs that in many ways are identical to our collective needs. We long for balance and belonging. We hunger for strength, wisdom and grace beyond ourselves to guide our minds in the way of peace.

We acknowledge the fact that it is only from God that we receive the food that supports the life of our earthly body as well as our heavenly body, the body of Christ. We are asked to break the bread of our lives with one another, living the example of God's presence. We are asked to keep watch for opportunities that God will provide, for they will surely come our way by grace. The bread we are to ask for is broken, and then shared. We too are broken, and then shared. This is our life in Christ. This is the living bread of our life in Christ Jesus.

5.   *"Forgive us our debts, as we also have forgiven our debtors."*

God is love. Jesus was sent by God to teach us of the love of God. On the way back to his Father, Jesus taught us that love is not complete if there is not forgiveness. Jesus on the cross, prayed to our Father in heaven to forgive those who had placed him there, because they did not know what they were doing. (Luke 23:43).

Through the course of our lives, each one of us has had a time to reflect, and wonder: what on earth was I thinking? We can remember having negative thoughts, leading to spoken words, causing harmful behavior, resulting in pain. Each one of us has been a receiver, as well as a source, of pain and tension. Tension results in destruction or in peaceful release. Jesus teaches us to take the way of peaceful release. Jesus would say forgive, because sometimes we do not know what on earth we are doing. Forgive them, and forgive yourself: take the life giving way of spiritual liberation found in the love and the will of God.

We are familiar with the numerous obstacles to forgiveness. God's grace does not pause at obstacles when our prayer-filled and spirit-filled consent to the will of God is at the front of our emotional choices. It is not so much within our power to forgive an offense, but each one's heart does have the capacity to be transformed when we can surrender to the belief that God wants to take each one of us a better way.

Through Jesus Christ, by the power of the Holy Spirit, there is a place where the reconciliation stands as mystical fact and the invitation to be there is unceasing. The grace of our daily bread is what sustains us as we pray to be the open, empty and receptive vessel for the grace of God's forgiveness. Love and forgiveness walk hand in hand in the ground of God, continually seeking their destiny as the dynamic evidence of God's presence in our world today, protecting us and preparing us for all that is to come. Forgiveness bears witness in our world that God's love is stronger than wrong, and completes the mission of Jesus in our hearts.

6. *"Do not bring us to the time of trial."*

When we look for completion in ways not in accordance with God's will, we are faced with temptation. We pray that God will not bring us to the time of trial for the choices we make, but will steer us in a better direction. The world is a compellingly attractive place. We can become disorganized, disordered in it. When this happens, we become tempted in ways not in accordance with God's will. There is a strong feeling component attached to temptation. We know how we feel when we are not centered in God. We know how we feel when we are centered in God. Every step we take is either away or toward our completion. Every step is our choice.

When we give in to temptation our response may be seen as coming out of our earthly nature from something in us that is unresolved. We are tempted to perpetuate a resentment, we are tempted to anger, to bodily harm by our ingestions; we are tempted by people, places and things in ways that are not in alignment with God's will. There is an attraction, excitement or an addiction with a false sense of completion that draws us. The focus for us must then become the issue within that represents to us our lack of fulfillment or true sense completion.

Rather than reacting when faced with temptation, we pray that we may be granted the grace of waiting: waiting for God's grace to grant us the insight and strength needed to restore us to spiritual

wisdom and liberation. Deeper understanding, not of the external
source of temptation, but of oneself is most relevant to our ongoing
deeper conversion to Christ.

There are many compelling voices competing for the sounds
of God in silence. God loves us all unspeakably much, and will
protect us. The voice of God is not likely the loudest voice we will
hear. We have good cause to remain open in our silent contemplation, trusting God's action to bring us toward completion. We
have received the privilege of God's grace: would we then choose
not to betray our salvation?

7.   *"Rescue us from the evil one."*

Evil is a reality that cannot be denied. Elements of evil can be
found from the beginning of time through all ages. Evil is seen in
natural disasters of fires, earthquakes, famine and floods, causing
human pain and destruction; evil is found in human nature, individually and collectively. Everywhere around us and within us there
are opposing forces. We can find ourselves in the painful middle of
a struggle to bear witness to what is right.

Anyone, anyplace, or anything that works against God's master
plan of peace and unity for all mankind falls into the category of
evil. The negative forces can remain nameless. To name them gives
undue credibility. Leaving anyone, anyplace, or anything nameless
diminishes power, honor and recognition. When we pray, we join
in a steady stream of prayer that has been in existence for over 2000
years, all by God's unending grace. As a part of God's master plan,
each one of us has been called by a new name by God giving power,
honor and recognition to us, and to all of the children of God.

Our God loves us where we are, and promises deliverance.
God protects us against opposing forces by drawing us into union
with one another in the Kingdom. Everything in life is preparation for what is to come. The preceding petitions of "The Lord's
Prayer" prepare, strengthen and sustain us in right order to pray
for God's protection from evil. There is an order to the petitions,

just as there is an order to life whereby we are strengthened by all of the blessings and trials of the past as they serve to prepare us for the present and for the future.

We are given opportunities in every moment to turn away or toward God. With God at our side, we are provided with an abundance of spiritual common sense. Through faith we are placed in a very powerful position, held in God's constant protection. Our confidence lies not in ourselves, but rather in the strength of our heavenly Father who loves and guides us through each day and toward all of our tomorrows. Our Father in heaven, by the power of the Holy Spirit, has sent his only Son to bless us and guide us along the way: the love, the sacrifice and the constant presence of Jesus in our lives is our reality that cannot be denied.

Even though I walk through the darkest valley, I fear no evil;
for you are with me. – Psalm 23:4

8.   *The Doxology*

For the kingdom, the power and the glory are yours
forever and ever.

Ours is the kingdom of new life, a kingdom that began with the grace of the birth of an infant in a stable, casting new light on the meaning of power, leading to the creation of an upside down notion of what a kingdom should be: a kingdom where less is better; loss is gain.

The kingdom of God includes the mysteries of the universe and the ground beneath our feet, and everything in between. Sometimes clouds of disappointment, sorrow and rejection block our sight; nevertheless, the sovereignty of the mountains remains. The clouds in our line of vision are filled with God's mercy and tenderness, ultimately sending down their showers of blessings.

We search for answers to the complex questions in life. We have options. Jesus teaches us to how to pray, and on the cross he teaches us why we pray. Jesus on the cross teaches us there is nowhere closer to our earthly sorrows than the kingdom, the power and the glory of God. The gospels are summarized here in these hours of Jesus on the cross: Jesus transcended suffering, for us. It is in our peaceful surrender to the glory and the power of the kingdom that we can begin to see life more fully from the center of our being. In so doing we experience an ever widening circle of serenity and stillness; the circle is one of infinite radius, without circumference.

Ours is a living faith, and our kingdom is a sending one. We are affected by the written word given to us in the sacred scriptures. Each one of us is called to translate the written word of God into action as we encounter others. On the road to Emmaus, the disciples were profoundly affected by face-to-face transmission of the word of God in their encounter with Jesus (Luke 24:13-35). We need to be open to the presence of Christ showing up in others when least expected and to remember: when I walk with another, there is my teacher. This is the real presence of Christ in the world today.

"As the Father has loved me, so I have loved you;
abide in my love." – John 15:9

THE BEATITUDES
Matthew 5:1-10

1. *Blessed are the poor in spirit, for theirs is the kingdom of heaven.*
2. *Blessed are those who mourn, for they will be comforted.*
3. *Blessed are the meek, for they will inherit the earth.*
4. *Blessed are those who hunger and thirst for righteousness, for they will be filled.*
5. *Blessed are the merciful, for they will receive mercy.*
6. *Blessed are the pure in heart, for they will see God.*
7. *Blessed are the peacemakers, for they will be called children of God.*
8. *Blessed are those who are persecuted for righteousness' sake, for theirs is the kingdom.*

1. "Blessed are the poor in spirit, for theirs is the kingdom of heaven."

Beatitude is finding wealth in all things of heavenly goodness from which nothing is missing. Jesus went up to the mountain to teach us beatitude from the place where all shadows are left behind, where the light comes from all sides, from the rays of the sun and from the light of truth. All darkness is away. In the light of Christ the Beatitudes reveal a complete order of heavenly beauty, grace and peace.

Jesus often spoke to us in parables, because the truth was not something we could readily receive or believe, but in the Beatitudes Jesus speaks to us directly: "Blessed are the poor in spirit, for theirs is the kingdom of heaven." A way to understand spiritual poverty is to consider its opposite: material possession. Material possession is apt to deceive the senses by giving a false sense of completion. Jesus teaches us that the poor are blessed and he grieves over the rich because they find their treasure in an abundance of goods. The rich and the full have no need. Jesus tells us hungry is better. Empty is better than full. If we are filled we have no need of God's grace. Even if we did, there would be no room. If I am filled with too many people, places and things, there is no room, and I cannot receive all that God has to give to me, which then is all that I have to give to others, because we can only give what we possess. Jesus points the way to the kingdom where the true inheritance can be found.

The most complete example of the first Beatitude is Jesus on the cross: the spiritual poverty sustained by Jesus up to and on the cross is difficult to reduce to just words. Jesus gave himself in complete spiritual poverty in order to receive the fullness of the blessing of the kingdom of God our Father. Jesus teaches us by word and example that, in our spiritual poverty, we have an unlimited capacity to be filled with the blessings of the kingdom of God: this is my inheritance, "For the Lord gives his blessing there, where he found the vessels empty" (Thomas á Kempis, *Imitation of Christ,* Bk XV Ch 3). In our openness, in our emptiness we are granted the grace to receive the blessings of the remaining seven Beatitudes.

2.   *"Blessed are those who mourn, for they will be comforted."*

Throughout all of history we have seen continual movement from desolation to consolation and back again, and again and ultimately forward. Life carries deep grief and pain. Life also brings very great consolation. God's love longs to touch us, heal us and make us whole. Sometimes in great sadness we pray to be granted the grace of waiting: waiting to feel the already presence of God's grace.

To mourn is to be fully human. Sometimes we mourn what we cannot even see or name, but know only that there is a cloud of darkness resulting in a feeling of darkness. I mourn my life. I mourn my transgressions; that is, all the mistakes I've ever made in this my life on earth. We mourn when we feel separated from someone, something or someplace we have loved. We mourn the death of someone we have loved; we mourn the death of someone we have yet to love. We mourn what was, and now is not. We seek constancy in our relationships and we seek constancy in our spiritual journey. Neither is to be found. Our faith is a faith feels cluttered with contradiction and opposites. Black shows up better by being placed next to white. We understand happiness more clearly when we know the darkness and the depth of sadness. The embrace of Jesus on the cross includes the extremes.

The spiritual journey is lived in one continuous thread from our conception to a natural death, but the continuous thread has many wayward and deviant moments in it. We experience doubt, despair, and the need to let go. Ours is a New Testament theology. We believe in the incarnation. God does not send us pain. God stands with us in the heartfelt center of our pain and sadness. When Jesus weeps over Jerusalem (Luke 19:41), it is not with a narrow embrace. In contemplative prayer, we wait to understand God. The mystical fact of our faith is that God already understands us. This is our contemplation: Jesus weeps, for me. It is here where I am consoled. It is here that I am blessed.

3. *"Blessed are the meek, for they will inherit the earth."*

The meek person is one who extends spiritual generosity to others by showing humility, gentleness, patience and tenderness. Take time; be gentle and be kind. A simple composure leads to our blessedness and enriches the lives of those around us. The one who is modest, reticent and observant does not make a mistake.

In contrast, our human nature can be very quick to turn toward wrong. When life does not appear to give to us what is wanted, we are brought to some measure of restlessness. I can either decide to move into higher gear to obtain what feels lost, or I can choose to be humble as Christ was humble. If I take the first route I perpetuate the cycle once again, exhaust myself even more, and find myself still disappointed with life. There is a way that will take us one step in the right direction, and that way is one of prayer. In heartfelt openness, in empty-handedness we allow obstacles to fall by the wayside. In contemplative prayer, in meekness of spirit, in the emptiness of spiritual poverty I meet God, because I can.

Subtraction is the math of Jesus. The focus is on God's strength, not mine; on God's will, not mine. The meek person of Jesus has an extensively powerful nature with great interior discipline, and lives a life in surrender to the will of God. Confessing my powerlessness is the first step to healing. When I am meek, I am willing to commit my life to the will of God.

God sent his only Son to earth to communicate with us of earthly nature. Jesus went to the highest mountain to teach us that the ground we stand on is holy; this is the ground that is our inheritance. This is our rightful blessedness. The meek shall inherit the earth, and this earth where we stand is holy ground. In spiritual poverty, void of earthly passions we come closer to our basic hunger and thirst for righteousness. This is the kingdom come to bless us on this day.

4.   *"Blessed are those who hunger and thirst for righteousness, for they will be filled."*

Righteous behavior carries elements of integrity and honesty. The attitudes of a righteous person are respectful and ethical, and one lives a life in conformity to the will of God. Jesus places righteousness in the same category as our basic needs for food and water. Jesus does not say grow into it when you are ready, because it's the right thing to do. Jesus instructs us to hunger for it now and to thirst for it now, as if life depends on it, and when we see it missing to feel the pain of its absence as if we have been deprived of food and water.

In contemplative prayer we are called to a very special kind of listening, a heart changing kind of listening. Jesus enters into our hearts in the silence of our prayer to free us from the poverty and self-absorption of our earthly passions and illusions. Jesus teaches us to live a life of justice and compassion not only within oneself, but ultimately and actively in relation to others.

Clarity is gained in prayer. The uncluttered mind can see through to the truth that is central to our existence: each one of us is equally loved and called precious in God's sight. Spiritual generosity feels effortless and right, for the good of the whole. When I follow my heart's clearest desires, keeping God at the center, my behavior remains well ordered in consideration of others.

When basic spiritual values are kept intact the righteous person will sense immediately whether something is right or wrong, and act on it. We are made of many parts, but one whole. Our wholeness does not make us our own entity. The message of Jesus is not personalized exclusively to our own special needs. We are each a person in process, committed to continuous transformation and conversion in relationship to others. Jesus came to make all things new: in the love and the light of Christ, I am not who I was (2 Corinthians 5:17). We pray that we may one day be judged on having lived life with an insatiable hunger and thirst for all that is pleasing in the eyes of God, for the good of the whole.

5. *"Blessed are the merciful, for they will receive mercy."*

Jesus has given us very clear instructions on how we are to live our lives: I am to love God, love my neighbor, and keep a forgiving heart. My neighbor is the one with whom I stand face to face in any given moment, and who offers me the opportunity to open my merciful heart.

Life in many ways is divided up into opposites. We may be hungry or full, rich or poor, quite sick or in good health, and filled with sadness or joy. In everything there is division. We experience the good things in life, or we are left wanting. Mercy is a voluntary sorrow and compassion that actively joins itself to the sufferings of those who are left wanting. The merciful heart keeps watch for those in need, overlooks the obstacles that could be perceived, and responds with kindness and compassion. Mercy is love and forgiveness enacted.

It is through prayer that our hearts become increasingly open to God's transforming grace. In prayer the way is cleared for God's grace to cultivate the soil of the heart for the garden of light. The light of God's grace gained in our prayer today is cumulative, and gradually becomes a natural extension of who we are, more and more of the time. Our God does not leave us wanting, but sometimes we turn in other ways. We are always called back.

In contemplation our hearts can be freed from earthly preoccupations, if only for a moment. In that moment, we may be granted the insight to see how the pieces of the puzzle of life fit together. God's mercy is a grace freely given, and as I believe this is so, then it is my loving and faith-filled responsibility to extend this gift to others. God grants us the grace of a merciful heart, a heart that is not indifferent to the needs of others, but one that can offer a kind word and sometimes so much more, a heart that can at the very least pray for whatever it cannot heal or rectify; a heart that cares as Jesus does.

6.   *"Blessed are the pure in heart, for they will see God."*

The heart is the whole focus of the teachings of Jesus. To be pure in heart is to be free of confused selfish intentions and self-seeking desires. Purity of heart can lead us to show up in life with one whole personality everywhere we go, and not this one here, and another one there. The one who is pure in heart sees all of life with clarity and simplicity, with no spare parts, as through the eyes of a child. In purity of heart, responses in life are clearly and effectively implemented, uncompromisingly so. So why is it so elusive?

We live in a non-tribal, individualist, technology-focused culture, and our behaviors and thought processes tend to continually pick up, in undiscerning fashion, what it is we are exposed to. Our balance can be found within for what is without. By going within, we are given contrast to external chaos and confusion. When we have contrast of opposites, we see two or more options with clarity, and it becomes clear that the outer contains varying levels of validity.

Contemplative prayer is our pause point, the point where we touch clarity and purity of heart and where, for a moment in time, we meet God and only God. A pianist walks out on to the stage, sits down at the keyboard, and pauses before beginning to play a Mozart sonata. The pause point is significant. It is a point most of us are inclined to skip; in any given interaction, we are more inclined to go directly from arrival to purpose. In the pause point of our prayer, all points come to one, and we become connected to our spiritual base with a clearly defined purpose. We touch, for a moment in time, the holy and stable ground of the roots of our common existence.

In the pause point of our prayer we are given a touchstone for clarity, stability, and purity of heart. We begin to see from an uncluttered perspective that all points do come to one for the good of the whole, and for a moment in time the world around us turns a little bit better.

7. *"Blessed are the peacemakers, for they will be called children of God."*

In war we close in on something; in peace we give space. Peace is deeper and richer than the absence of war. Peace is the tranquility of order. Order is grounded in harmony and balance. Peace is the effect of a merciful and charitable heart. Peace is the work of justice. Jesus desires to fill our hearts and grants us the grace of his peace, then instructs us to go and bear witness in a world where there is pain and tension.

Peace generates peace. Conflict and contention generate conflict and contention. When we feel flooded with the tensions of conflict we have the option to seek a higher ground, the enduring ground of God's grace found in many ways and particularly in prayer. To be at peace is to experience an alignment with a greater purpose beyond oneself, so that one's life can be an effortless yet powerful act of blessing and a force for good in the world. The one who brings peace to another has found peace within, because we can only give what we know and possess.

Our values are ordered in two ways, by our human nature and by our spiritual nature; God calls us to one. In the order of the Beatitudes, Jesus shows us the unfettered pathway of peace. Jesus does not speak to us in aimless fashion. The words of Jesus are well intended and in right order. Jesus meets us in our poverty of Spirit, where we find comfort in our rightful inheritance, filled with a hunger for all that is good in the eyes of God, and a desire for peace that does not pause at obstacles. Though we may have good health, a home and profitable work, if peace is missing, then our days feel incomplete. Every step we take is either away or toward our completion; every step is our choice. Jesus says go and bear witness, take the way of peaceful release and spiritual liberation, and you will find rest for your souls (Matthew 11:28).

8.   *"Blessed are those who are persecuted for righteousness' sake, for theirs is the kingdom."*

To live a righteous life means that we are living a spiritual life consistent with the standards of what is right and just, according to our central values. To suffer persecution means that we experience the painfully unacceptable behavior of others for doing so, causing us suffering. In our suffering we long for a felt sense of balance and belonging. We begin to question: do I belong there? Or here? Or where? Jesus says: "Come unto me" (Matthew 11:28).

Jesus understands opposing forces and the polarities of human nature. Opposing forces are around us, and within us. There are many voices in the world that want to speak over the voice of Jesus. Our choice is to actively engage, or to give time and space wherein the Holy Spirit can live and move and breathe. Persecution carries the power to take us to a deeper center within ourselves where, within our suffering, we meet God. In our prayer we may be granted the grace to begin to yield to God's mysterious purpose. In our deepest center God replaces pain with grace and strength.

Contemplation of all these things can bring balance into our lives, connecting the pain of human suffering with the divine presence of God. Our journey on earth is mysterious and profound. In the silence of our prayer, we become aware that contemplative spirituality is so much more than a thin stream of consciousness reserved for a select few. Along the way, we discover the pathway to a full-bodied spirituality, grounded in the Body of Christ. We stay faithful to our course because we cannot compromise our values, even in the face of estrangement and rejection. We are not asked to seek approval or justification. We are asked to stay honest. We remain steadfast in our gentleness. Through faith we believe there is strength greater than ours, longing to bring us toward wholeness, toward holiness, and our response is our *yes*. To this God stands pleased. "Blessed are you … Rejoice and be glad, for your reward is great in heaven" (Matthew 5:11-12).

The Prayer of St. Francis

1.   *Lord, make me an instrument of your peace.*
2.   *Where there is hatred, let me sow love*
3.   *Where there is injury, let me sow pardon*
4.   *Where there is doubt, let me sow faith*
5.   *Where there is despair, let me sow hope*
6.   *Where there is darkness, let me sow light*
7.   *And where there is sadness, let me sow joy*
8.   *O Divine Master*
9.   *Grant that I may not seek so much to be consoled, as to console, to be understood, as to understand*
10. *To be loved, as to love with all my soul*
11. *For it is in giving that we receive, and it is in forgiving that we are forgiven*
12. *And it is in dying that we are born to eternal life*

1.   *Lord, make me an instrument of your peace.*

When in prayer St. Francis heard a voice coming from the crucifix saying to him three times: "Francis, go and repair my house, which you can see is falling down." Those repairs led him to his passion of service to all of creation.

An instrument is a means by which something is accomplished. An instrument is also capable of producing music, that is beauty, harmony and balance. Music is made up of notes and rests, sounds and silence. The rest is the space between notes, and tones are neither played nor sung into the rest. Contemplation is our rest between the notes of life.

Music has been called the universal language. There has never been a culture that existed without some form of musical expression, and as such music is one of the keys to understanding our existence, both individually and collectively. In the world of St. Francis there were no machines, none of the background noises of modern life, and no ways to reproduce sound from its purest source. The direct experience of music was a life force of harmony and balance.

Where there is balance and harmony, there is peace. Where there is peace, there is rest. Peace is our universal desire. To be an instrument of God's peace means first of all to know the source and direct experience of God's peace within me, so that I can then be an instrument of God's peace in relationship to others. That is to say that I can then begin to make repairs in the house, which I can see is falling down, beginning with my own.

At the close of life, Francis challenged his followers: I have done my part; may God now help you to do yours. When we pray, "Lord, make me an instrument of your peace" we are bowing down before God's skill as creator, as Master Musician, as Composer of all of our days.

2. *Where there is hatred, let me sow love.*

We are the blessed vessels of God's love here on earth. The love of God is dynamic and perpetually seeks a dwelling place, leading us to walk in the way of inspiration. God sent his son Jesus to teach us the way we should go. Jesus shows us human acts of God's love. The Holy Spirit sows the seeds of the possibilities of the Love of God on earth. In truth, nothing draws us quite as powerfully as love. Where I am loved, I'll go. Each day, one foot in front of the other, like in the meditation walk, decisions are made out of preference for the light and the love of Christ, or we walk another way. Jesus says: "follow me" (Luke 9:23).

St. Francis understands the human heart in knowing that love is stronger than hate. Hatred is a consuming negative force coming from an empty center. At its core is loneliness and deep hurt, with perhaps an unknown longing to be freed from the bonds of self-absorption. Love, even the most fragile love, can conquer hate because in truth the emptiness waits to be filled.

If we deny the love within us, or only partially live it out, then we are only partially alive. We are refusing to trust in the power of love that is within us. By turning away we are allowing some aspect of creation in the world around us to travel a little further down the road of darkness. The farther we travel down a certain path in life, the more that path shapes us and affects our heart and spirit. If we set our feet upon the path of darkness, we will walk into darkness. If we set our feet on the road to light, we will walk toward the light. It is a fundamental law of human nature and all of creation.

Ours is a God who loves us where we are. God meets us in our deepest need and will not leave us wanting. God sent the Holy Spirit to scatter the seeds of possibility of the love that is known in every human heart. Each day, a thousand times and in a thousand ways, we are called upon to make a choice that will incline us either toward the darkness of hatred or toward the light and the transforming love of God where the pathway is made clear. The crown of God has many jewels; stretch out your hand and release the one you are holding.

3.   *Where there is injury, let me sow pardon.*

Pardon carries the potential of leading to healing. When we pray "let me sow pardon" we pray to be granted the grace to be the one to seek healing and reconciliation. Francis calls us to sow the seeds; the seeds are the seeds of possibility, which means further growth may come. With seeds not sowed, things are inclined to remain stuck; the door remains closed. When by the grace of God seeds can be sown, then we can lean in the direction of healing.

There is an image of two people pulling on opposite ends of a rope, creating tension. If one lets go, the tension ceases to exist. Does the weaker let go? Or does the stronger let go? It is everyone's desire to move forward. I can wait for another to take the first step, or I can draw on the strength of taking the initiative.

We are not asked to seek approval, justification, or solutions. We are asked to stay honest, and to take one step in the right direction to restore health to body, mind and spirit. Contemplative prayer serves the purpose of connecting the pain of human suffering with the divine presence of God. Through prayer we begin to yield to God's mysterious purpose. When I take one small step, I stand in a different position. My perceptions are changed. When my perceptions are changed, my heart is changed. Through faith, we believe there is a strength greater than ours, longing to bring us toward wholeness, toward holiness.

At our base we are all vulnerable to pain, to injury. We have been injured; we have given injury. We carry pain individually, and we carry pain collectively. We are invited to see a way to touch a situation so that it does not remain in a stuck position. Acknowledge; sow the seeds of pardon, then wait, and watch for God's intervening grace. We call this shift the first step toward healing. Entrust the rest to God. With the seeds of pardon planted, the flower of true forgiveness may bloom one day.

4. *Where there is doubt, let me sow faith.*

When did I doubt God was at my side? At what point did I begin to see things differently? When did it dawn in my consciousness that God stands with me in my deepest center, even in my fears and doubts, and when I cannot see? More often, such growth in awareness of God's presence is seen in retrospect: I can see it now, but I could not see it then. We can take such spiritual truths from our past and apply them to our present in times when we cannot see.

Faith comes to take away our doubt. Faith came to St. Paul on the road to Damascus, and he was literally knocked to the ground with a truth that he could not in any part deny (Acts 9:1-6). Faith is not always so dramatic. Faith is more often subtle yet incessant in quietly shaping our insights and responses to life. Where there is doubt, we pray to sow the seeds of our faith. We do not use our awareness to put others on the path, but from our deepest heartfelt honesty we can point to the path, knowing full well the truth of its existence. The rest is up to God, who always works in mysterious ways, and who has all things in hand.

We all have differing gifts. Instead of telling or explaining seed by seed the ways of my growth in faith, there is another way most visible and effective, and that is to simply live it generously with every encounter. Spiritual generosity takes many forms and will usually find a way out at the right time, in the right place if we do not stand in our own way, and when we trust in God's providence to influence us.

God leads us to live each day in the faithful heartfelt simplicity of love and forgiveness. Jesus shows us the way. The Holy Spirit is our dynamic source of inspiration, weaving together all goodness. In contemplation we remain open to the dynamic evidence of God's threefold presence, reminding us that in truth the orderliness of heaven cannot be disturbed.

5.   *Where there is despair, let me sow hope.*

When my sense of self becomes dependent on what I can acquire and produce, my desires become frustrated and I become distracted by disappointment and despair. The pathway to spiritual liberation is slowed. When a person feels overcome with despair, it seems as if there is no word of consolation that can be meaningful. And yet, God remains in all wordlessness.

When there is despair, the ground of my being can feel dark and hazy. There is some measure of inertia. When there is inertia, my vision is limited. When my vision is limited there is self-absorption, which is often unrecognized. My foundation feels shaky because it is. Authenticity slips away. I have become my dilemma.

There is a better way, and there is another voice. There is another part, the silent part. With practiced attentiveness to the silent presence of God, we become grounded in a foundation that is stronger than any of our involuntary weaknesses: the ground of God found in prayer. Where there is despair, God is more than merely present. In truth, our God of compassion stands in the deepest center of the despairing heart. In contrast, the inertia of despair does not have the vitality to take up roots in my heart.

As my foundation in the ground of God grows stronger, in reality by comparison the ground of negativity is weakened. We may or may not get past something that feels impossible, but we may be able to begin to see that it is not our whole life. It is the lesser part. When the despairing soul is to heal, it will do so on its own, by the grace of God and in God's time.

The greatest gift we have to offer to another is our selfless and solitary witness. For when we stand vigil with the despairing spirit, more than anything else we are denying the emptiness into which the human spirit may dare to descend. We offer the simple presence of the Spirit of hope that refuses to withdraw. We bear witness to the fact that Love is closer and stronger than wrong.

6. *Where there is darkness, let me sow light.*

Because of his very great faith, St. Francis was knowingly and unknowingly able to touch others. When for a brief moment someone is able to break through and affect us, it can seem like a ray of sunlight has filled our entire heart. We know in that moment that we are alive, and that our heart has the capacity to heal. Having found the source within, each of us has the capacity to knowingly and unknowingly affect another.

St. Francis does not call us to be the light; he asks us to sow seeds of the light. God will be the light. We are not the way. We are not the way, the truth and the light. God is. We are but a brief reflection of the light of a truth greater than any of us. Our role is to offer illumination as we can in the darkness that surrounds us, even when we ourselves may feel engulfed by it. Francis knew darkness. He felt the pain of the beggar and the leper. He was tormented by rejection, with bodily illness, and a desire for a conventional life. In his pain he was touched at a deeper level, and out of the depths he was able to reflect the light.

When our days seem to be too long and too dark, sometimes the worst of a situation is that we feel alone in it. We can become anxious in darkness because we cannot see, and it appears as if nothing is happening. This may be a time to remember that in the beginning, all of the seeds planted by God are dormant and in darkness. For seeds, darkness is necessary for germination. The darkness creates in us an emptiness that is capable of being filled with the light of Christ. The light of Christ brings all things to new life.

Where there is darkness, very often there is my teacher. When it appears as if nothing is happening, something is. Our sense of the light may be faint and fragile; in truth, against even the smallest of lights, the darkness cannot stand. It is altered and my perceptions are changed. When my perceptions are changed, my heart is changed, and my behavior follows my heart.

The world is a strange and mysterious mix of darkness and light. It is not our task to judge the worthiness of our own light. In the physics of the spiritual life, our actions set off other actions beyond our capacity to know, predict or imagine, and there the darkness is altered the light of God's grace.

7.   *Where there is sadness, let me sow joy.*

Sadness carries a "was-ness" about it. Or perhaps it carries an "if only" about it. Something or someone was significant and now is missing or has yet to come. There is a void with a feeling of brokenness. In the brokenness, there is a crack in my heart. The crack forms an opening. It is the nature of water to sink to the lowest place; my tears fall into the open broken place in my heart where God has long ago sown the seeds of joy. Watered by grace, the seeds very gradually begin to show signs of new life. One tear bears silent solitary witness to the fact that God's grace longs to touch us, to heal us and to love us toward all of our tomorrows. In my tears there is a softening of heart, a sign of God's grace. Broken-hearted gradually becomes open-hearted.

God's grace of the solitary tear does not get taken back. When there is a felt sense of the absence of grace, one of us has walked away. The invitation to walk back is unceasing. In the grace of the tear, God grants us the grace of compassion: by way of our own needs, we know the needs of another. Because there is a need for us to do so, God will grant us the grace to be present to another. We each have the capacity to be present to another with a tender desire to nurture the saddened heart. We are aware of pain and suffering in the world. With our intent to sow seeds of joy, we enter into the sadness of another. In sharing the joy of transformation, we are raising awareness of beauty, kindness and spiritual generosity.

We are so conditioned to think that our life revolves around great moments, and yet in truth our life revolves around the silent subtleties of the human heart. By faith and God's grace, sadness gradually transforms into joy. Joy is silent, and it is subtle. Joy has a sense of simplicity about it. Joy is from deep within. There is sweet surrender when our tears of sorrow mingle with the inspiration of the Holy Spirit, and the seeds of joy begin to flower in the garden of God's delight.

8.   O Divine Master

Francis was often with many. Song was their traveling companion. Against all obstacles, Francis continued to sing the divine praises of God along the highways of life. For Francis his whole life became the seed, scattered and sown, trusting in the joyful compassionate Spirit of our Divine Master to bring new life from the soil of completion.

When the farmer goes out to sow, some seeds fall by the wayside, some on stone or among the thorns, and some on good soil, yielding a beautiful harvest (Mark 4:4-12). None of us can predict what will happen, but we can shape our intentions. Francis found spiritual freedom in the joyful outward expression of the perpetual and the dynamic love of God. Francis did not appear to be attached to outcomes; he walked in the way of inspiration, trusting in God to guide him.

Along the way, Francis was seen by some to be too free and loose in his ways. Some considered him to be haphazard; others felt he was too trusting in God. Francis knew the polarities of human nature. He experienced human hatred, injury, doubt, despair, darkness and sadness. With the strength of his Divine Master, who is ours, Francis experienced conversion from negativity to love, pardon, faith, hope, light and joy. For Francis, it became a holy requirement to die to the opinions of others, beginning with his father from whom he became separated. His response was as clear as the one Jesus gave to his mother: "Did you not know that I must be in my Father's house?" (Luke 2:49).

Prayer is not separated from our actions. Every encounter holds the advent of God's blessing, and each one of us carries enormous potential beyond our present experience. Together in faith we know where we are going. In prayer it can seem as if the soul is doing nothing, when in truth our Divine Master is doing very much. Contemplation opens us to the fullness of God's grace. We can learn that even in our darkest hour our Divine Master will use us as an instrument of grace and peace to bring love and consolation to those we meet along the highways of life.

9.   *Grant that I may not seek so much to be consoled as to console, to be understood as to understand.*

In certain precious moments we are not left wanting. Precious moments are often found in an encounter with another person, or in nature, and in prayer. We experience consolation and understanding in the purest sense. We know we have been met. Does it feel possible to look back and say God was there too?

Ours is an incarnation theology; our faith lives within us. God's grace cannot be kept contained, and will show up in ways both known and unknown to us in any given moment. God longs to touch us, to heal us, to make us whole and will do so directly, and indirectly through others. There are certain times when we encounter another person, or when we encounter God in prayer, and we notice as a result that life has clearly taken a turn for the better. We feel less boxed in and we can see beyond our limitations to new horizons. We feel consoled. We feel understood.

We are all more alike than we are different. The spiritual journey is a lifelong one with movement from consolation to desolation and then back again, and ultimately forward. Each one of us goes through the trials of life with the refinement of grace at the center, meeting our God who guides us through all things. We come to know that all of our accumulated shortcomings, no matter how numerous, are not more powerful than God's grace.

God's grace can bring a sense of wholeness, and perhaps of completion. There may be a felt body sense of openness, consolation and understanding. Consolation and understanding walk hand in hand with gratitude in the ground of God found in prayer. We become familiar with the paradoxical mystical fact that gifts from God are for keeps, and gifts from God are bound for giving away. I have received from God a heart of consolation and understanding; this then is what I have to give. God invites us to be observant. God invites us to be opportunistic.

10.   Grant that I may seek not so much as to be loved, as to love with all my soul.

Love unites us with God and with one another. With our heart-felt consent, love defines our course in life. It is by love that we have all been sanctified, and it is in sanctification that all creatures have potential for renewal and new vitality in Jesus Christ. The spiritual magic of Francis is that love always felt new, refreshed in its expression to all who crossed his path, and to all of creation.

Love is a quiet dynamic force that perpetually seeks multiplication. By giving love, love was reflected back to St. Francis, magnified many times by God's grace. This is the wonderful arithmetic of God's love. By giving love, rather than for waiting for love to break down our barriers, we find that the chains of our self-installed barriers are broken away. If we feel ourselves engulfed in the darkness of our loneliness and self-absorption, our first act need not be to call out for someone to love us, but to seek a direction for the love God has placed in us.

Love is a quietly moving force perpetually seeking a dwelling place. The mission of love is to set the world on a better course by canceling innumerable wrongs. Our love in God has no judgment; it is freely given without regard for mistakes of the past. Love asks neither recognition nor reward and bears no attachment to outcomes, but is with us in the present moment, directing the actions of our soul and guiding our feet to a better way. We are not attached to yesterday, neither are we attached to tomorrow: God has loved us into the present moment. The love of today knows no impossibilities, because it knows no bounds. Love will fill the vessel of our own need, at the same time as it fills the heart of another and expands into spaces beyond, having implications way beyond our knowing. And besides, how do I want to be remembered?

11.   *For it is in giving that we receive, and forgiving that we are forgiven.*

Our bodies are nourished by food and water; our spirits are nourished by giving and forgiving. This is not high-minded spirituality, but a simple truth about the way the energy of life flows from one vibrant being to another and back again. The giver, the forgiver and the forgiven are released, yet bound by grace, and the original gift is multiplied many times.

St. Francis had the experience of coming face to face with a leper. He witnessed, and then he kissed the open wounds. It is easy to imagine that his action was not preceded by careful analytical thought. From a place of spiritual liberation, he was inspired by God's grace and compassion to live a life of spiritual generosity.

In contrast, when our thoughts keep us chained to issues that are from the past, we not only remain bound to the uninvited guest of our self-absorption, which is self-defeating, but we are chained to an interpretation of the world that closes doors on the miracles of possibility. When we give, and when we forgive we are opening the doors of possibility in a way that allows the love of Christ to shine through. In the light of the love of Christ, miracles can happen.

God loves all of us equally and impossibly much, and has given us a fairly level playing field. When we have the courage to trust in the heart felt action of the grace of forgiveness, and when we do not see this action as a diminishing of our own resources, then we will know one of the greatest secrets of life: it is in giving that we receive, and in forgiving that we are forgiven. In the knowing the secret, we know what it means to be rich.

Giving and forgiving perhaps bring us the closest we can come to bestowing God's divine grace on one another. We learn that nothing we can do will ever compare with the gift we give, or receive, when a human heart can say, "It's all OK." For in that moment, we feel a touch upon our spirit that, for all the world, feels like a blessing from the hand of God.

12. *For it is in dying that we are born to eternal life.*

To a person without conversion to Christ, death is death. To a person who has undergone conversion, death is the way to new life eternal. Death comes to us in many ways besides the obvious. Through the course of our prayer life, we come face to face with the overall goodness of God.

With the wisdom and the light that shines into our hearts through prayer, we also come face to face with parts of ourselves that no longer serve a healthy or useful purpose. By the generous light of God's grace, we can learn that we carry a whole cast of characters within us, with many different temperaments and personalities, altogether worthy of a Shakespeare cast. Some of them are genuine, granted by grace. Others of them remain attached to negative roots and the opinions of others. When we let fall away the negative roots and the opinions of others, and follow only the goodness within, then we can begin to know the true nature of spiritual liberation.

God calls us to a life of joy with internal simplicity in one continuous thread, beginning at our conception and lasting into eternity. This is the place where the reconciliation of all things

stands as mystical fact. Every moment brings opportunity for newness of life within us. Jesus taught us in the way of opposites and
paradox. Francis teaches this way too, calling us to let go of the
obstacles and let God be the Master Builder and Composer of all
of our days. It is as if Francis is asking us: Why would you want to
wait to live the joyful generosity of God's love for you? At the close
of his earthly life St. Francis gave us his final instructions: "I have
done my part; may Christ now teach you to do yours."

SPIRITUAL FRIENDSHIP

1. Spiritual Friendship
2. The Art of Compassion
3. The Simplest Expression
4. The Mystery of Joy
5. Exploring the Mystery
6. Conflict and the Light
7. Magnify the Lord
8. The Art of Leisure
9. Deepest Longings
10. Wildflowers
11. Heartbeat of the Parish
12. Preferring Christ

"I have called you friends, because I have made known to you everything that I have heard from my Father." – John 15:15

1. Spiritual Friendship

We have learned as Christians that we are created for union with God. We may see that union as an eventuality, or a way off into the distant future kind of "pie in the sky by and by when you die" kind of union. There are times when we long for our relationship with God to be a deeper one now, shared in relationship to one another.

Life brings us many challenges. Everyone has something in life they wish was a little easier, a little lighter, and less painful. Sometimes the worst of a situation can be that we feel alone in it. As we are drawn more and more into crowded and condensed spatial relationships, culturally speaking, the paradox is that we may actually feel that we have become more isolated. Sometimes we wonder where on earth we belong. Spiritual isolation could be considered the social disease of our era.

God meets us in our deepest need. Spiritual wilderness transcends all time, and yet out of it can come our deepest knowing of God's grace. When our days have become too long and too dark, we can learn that another can hold the light of love and compassion with us. In the light of God's presence, our awareness changes. We come to realize more clearly the spiritual nature of the friendship, in keeping with the promise of Jesus: "For where two or three are gathered in my name, I am there among them" (Matthew 18:20). Just as we grow to know and trust that another is here for us, we know too that God is here for us unconditionally and forever, because God does not leave us orphaned (Isaiah 43:1).

The inward journey can be a lonely one, but it need not be. Every relationship carries spiritual significance beyond what is obvious. It is in relationship to one another that we are awakened to a larger dimension of life. Spiritual friendship can be a way of deepening our relationship with God and with one another, a time to drop all effort and competition, and a time to find new freshness and openness to carry back to our outer life. Jesus calls us friends (John 15:15). Good friends leave us indentured: such sweet charity. Who is your spiritual friend? Thank him or her and wonder at how the relationship might be deepened. Who could be?

2. *The Art of Compassion*

Anyone with a deep commitment to the inner way has learned there are times when we experience clarity and growth, and other times when the inner world seems dark and confusing. As followers of Jesus we are given the opportunity to realize an intimate source of "I'll be there for you" kind of promise. In spiritual friendship we are encouraged to engage in the mysterious unfolding of our own story. We begin to see more clearly the relationship between God's call and our own "I am" as defined by St. Paul: "But by the grace of God I am what I am, and his grace toward me has not been in vain" (1 Corinthians 15:10).

There are times when we come together in joyful thanksgiving to share the good news of our lives. There are other times when the news feels otherwise and we bear the chains of our self-absorption in confusion and despair. In such times of darkness, to be with another confessing our powerlessness in silence, and to wait quietly on God's grace can be the truest gift of the heart in a relationship. Each of us holds the capacity to wait. In our waiting we are granted the grace to be present to the other, to listen and bear witness to the fact that each one of us is loved and called precious in God's sight. To be with another in the silence and stillness of unspoken prayer, or in conversation over a cup of tea can be quite a generous gift of the heart. We confess our powerlessness in the face of mystery. We return to our God centeredness. We begin to yield to a purpose greater than our own.

Compassion stands not alone but continually seeks expression in clear, simple and direct ways. Still waters of a pond become muddied and unclear when stirred by the oars of a boat, or by rocks thrown to sink to the mud bottom. In active and unclear waters the sky and trees cannot be reflected back to us; neither can we see to the bottom of things. By waiting in stillness we can begin to see through to the depth more clearly, and life can be reflected back to us. It is not too long to wait on God. In our waiting, we begin to experience clarity in our outer life and we can begin to see the ground of God's design more clearly. Our lives can be called compassion made manifest, by the grace of God.

3. *The Simplest Expression*

Spiritual friendship can be a connecting link between community worship and our individual prayer time. We can be a source of strength and encouragement to one another as we seek to grow more deeply into the ground of God found in our prayer. A way of praying that is particularly appropriate to the complexities of the times in which we live is contemplative prayer, sometimes called the prayer of the quiet, also known as the "simplest expression of the mystery of prayer" (*Catechism of the Catholic Church* N. 2713). Contemplative prayer is very simply stillness of mind and body in the presence of God. In the quiet, we create time in our life and space in our hearts in order to be with the perpetually refining grace of God's love.

Contemplative prayer is my nothingness before God's everythingness. Every life has creative potential beyond our present experience, and we trust in God's providence. Everyone's prayer experience is unique. There is no good, better or best way to pray. In humility and simplicity, we accept the gifts of God's love and grace that come to us along the way. Just for now we let go of the concerns of our hearts: all the people, places and things of our active life. It may be sufficient to pray: Lord I am here for you, and I know that you are here for me too.

To pray alone in one's room and, at other times, to be strengthened by the silent prayer of two or more together can be the simplest expression of our "yes" to God's grace. By our natural quiet state, we profess our openness to God's will, trusting that perhaps God wants to get a word in edgewise into our very active lives.

God finds us where we seek him: through our friendships, in community worship, in nature, and in the fertile holy ground of our prayer. To move forward in life without praying or listening to God means only to grow increasingly outward with no substantial base. A tree can grow in rocky soil, because the roots will find the way to bring living water to the tree. Without the roots finding the opening the tree would cease to exist. In our prayer we create inner space into which the Spirit of God can live, and move and breathe. Our roots become established in the stable and holy ground of God's grace. We stay grounded in the process of prayer, rather than attached to outcomes. We remain rooted in the ground of God for the good of the whole, for goodness' sake.

4.   *The Mystery of Joy*

Ours is a God who comes. God came to us in the beginning of time, transforming void into being and darkness into light. Our God comes today in our hearts, in our relationships and in all of nature. Just as faithfully as the sun rises up out of the desert each morning and sinks into the ocean at night, God comes to us in our hearts and in all of creation.

There are times when we experience the nearness of God. We know joy in its purest sense. We know in clear and simple ways that we are loved as a precious treasure in the hand of God (Isaiah 62:3). And yet there are other times when we may be as near to God as the bubble is to the ocean and still not know, not see. We could miss it. Yet there it is: a microcosm of joy, quiet and subtle (have you ever seen a noisy or a sad bubble?) floating along in the greatest of turbulence in perfect peace. And so often it is that way with joy, especially when we are grown: we could miss it.

Children access their joy so easily and naturally, and we delight in their spontaneity. In order to be a better guide for them, maybe we need to travel that way ourselves a little more frequently. In our later years the experience of joy is all too often limited to the interior. Maybe the deepest spiritual counterpart to joy has a quieter sense to it. Even so, we are astonished when in a flash of insight there are times when we too can move in childlike fashion from confusion to clarification with an infusion of joy. The gift of joy comes today and stands above all else, silent and unseen in every new moment in time. It is a gift we share with one another in relationship, by the grace of God for all of time.

The journey can be a lonely one, but it need not be. As difficult as it is to reduce the spiritual experience to mere words, we can gain insight into our own spiritual journey by articulating it to another. Joy becomes twice given when shared with another in spiritual friendship. This is the bliss of God's mystical arithmetic. This is where we are given precious bread for the journey.

5.   *Exploring the Mystery*

In our sophisticated world of technical enlightenment, power points, and incessant auditory and visual stimulation, we can sometimes lose track of the childlike grace to wonder, ponder and daydream. It takes time to stop to appreciate an encounter with another or a special moment in nature, or to ponder the mystery deep within our own hearts. Children know the art of leisure and daydreaming. Children have a special gift for cherishing the joy of exploration, and unknowingly unraveling mystery. Maybe it's out of our envy that we so often tell them to hurry. Jesus blesses the children, and tells us that when we become like them, the kingdom will be ours (Mark 10:15).

Life is mystery in many ways. Mystery is the dynamic side of reality and engenders paradox. Mystery is destined to be very slowly unfolded and partially revealed; discovery and revelation come in God's time. There is in each of us an inner mystery we will never fathom, and there is an interpersonal one too. So often we expect the show to start as soon as we get out of this relationship or into that one, or we get another degree, or that next big promotion and the salary goes up. One of these days we could wake up and realize that was life, and we missed it. Life is a continual process of mystery unfolding before our very eyes. We need not wait for God's work to begin: this is God's kingdom come.

As we take time to ponder the mystery of our life, we begin to accept that we can't know, or even understand everything. Some things are just plain unfigureoutable. The puzzling and painful situations in life put us in touch with the need for our Savior, who alone reveals to us page by page the mystery of our personhood. Each of us, though haunted by our own limits and imperfections, possesses enormous potential. Each one of us bears an immense capacity to change. It is a challenge to take time to wonder, ponder, and daydream, and it is an even greater challenge to reveal oneself to another in spiritual friendship. And yet with each revelation, a spiritual connection is made and another miracle takes place: God's kingdom comes.

6.   *Conflict and the Light*

Crisis and conflict, when they come, can bring the power to turn us into God's frozen chosen. We don't like to admit it, but we experience immobilization of thought and our actions can shut down too. All consolation evaporates. We long for a sharp and accurate focus, and any sense of direction. It is as if a broad band of bad feeling has come over us, and what a lonely feeling it can be, especially since it often comes in the dark of the night: here I am, meeting my own deepest nature, and I cannot not run and hide.

We seek a life of authenticity and substance and here in our fears we find light and a piece of truth. The problem to us, and the problem is a painful one, is that our awareness often comes in the form of conflict of emotions. Conflict engenders fire, the fire of affects and emotions, and like every fire it has two aspects, that of combustion and destruction and that of creating light. The combustion and destruction make a lot of noise. The light is quiet and it is healing. It can be difficult to see the light when we are so conscious of the destruction.

Nothing exists without its opposite; everything has a beginning, middle and an end. As aware as we all are of the conflict points in our lives, it is especially important that we not miss the complete picture, one of darkness and of light. Just as the pendulum of a clock swings toward balance, so does human nature. In both instances perfect balance is found, but not kept as the movement continues.

If one could forecast emotional weather it would probably be done with low accuracy and high variability. For the spiritual forecast the only certainty is change; this is our consolation. God speaks into the stillness of our point of balance, and asks us to remain a little while. God's love longs to touch us in precisely these kinds of places that are the most difficult and painful. God's love longs to heal us individually and collectively. Tension cannot sustain itself, and will eventually yield to the deeper truth of release and rest. Memory may serve us well: I have memory of being in this place before, and I came out of it. The light did come, and will come again. I expect that once again God's grace will intervene. God does not send us pain. God will stand with us in the heartfelt center of our pain, to live with us in this open wound of love. In so doing, the light does shine. It is the light of divine compassion. We do tend toward balance. And who are we for one another in this mysterious process of the journey of faith? By God's grace, we are friend.

7. *Magnify the Lord*

Mary mother of Jesus receives astonishing news and her response to God's word is clear, unique and specific: "My soul magnifies the Lord, and my spirit rejoices in God my Savior" (Luke 1:46). Mary magnifies the Lord. She magnifies the present. It can be a powerful force in our life, to magnify the Lord. Daily. Hourly. Moment to moment. Mary magnifies the Lord. Does she see the complete picture? One that includes sorrow, suffering and death on the cross? One that includes resurrection?

In our lifetime, here and now in this generation, we magnify many things with no particular instruction to do so. If the past was rosier than the present, then it can be a lot of fun to reflect on that, but it too is gone. We are under no special advisement to magnify our past or our present problems, and yet we so easily fall to doing this. We magnify the past, which for one thing is gone, and for another, if it was a difficult road we walked and we magnify that we could be defeated and depressed forever. In truth, our savior has freed us from the finite complexities of the past.

The season of Lent, like the season of spring, appeals not only to the heart and intellect but also to the senses. Our gifts of sight, taste, touch and smell can lead us to appreciate all facets of God's creation. Ashes, oil, palms, lilies, fire, incense and the baptismal waters of new life speak to our entire sense of being as we come to know more clearly the bread of life. We are surrounded by symbols calling to us to magnify the present moment, to magnify the Lord today in our hearts, in all of our behavior, in our work and in all of our relationships.

Today is ours, magnified by the light of our Lord and Savior Jesus Christ in the freedom of our faith. It is by the light and our new life in Christ that each one us of can say: I am not who I was. Today is what we have, and today is pregnant with possibilities for new life. We magnify many things in our lifetime. It is a choice we make daily. We will know by the fruits how our magnification process is working for us. How fruitful and powerful is your magnification process?

8.   *The Art of Leisure*

The commitments and distractions of daily life can often interfere with an inner knowing of who we are. We can spend so much time going outside to get fulfilled, to get paid, to catch up, then to get ahead that we often do not take the time to get to know the one who walks in our shoes. The effect is that if I am a stranger to myself, then I am also a stranger to others, beginning with my closest relationships.

Culture depends for its very existence on leisure. There has never been a culture that existed without art and music, and some sense of spiritual insight. Friendships, simple exercise and recreation, good deeds and spirituality begin to reflect basic well-ordered pleasures. Maybe there is temptation to not only smell the roses, but to stop and look at them too. Maybe there is room for leisure. When my life is brought into balance, I feel less a stranger to myself, and so then I am less a stranger to you also. I have a greater availability to all of life, and I welcome your friendship.

Leisure can be an attitude toward life, a condition of the soul, as much as it can be a block of spare time or a vacation away. Each of us is free in every moment to make personal decisions to live a life of balance, authenticity and substance. We seek new ways of fulfillment unrelated to the corporate world and financial success. When we are in relationship to the true center of our existence, we begin to experience balance and harmony in our outer relationships. Our work and possessions become the things that embellish and adorn our lives, but we are not centered in them. As we let our hearts rest in nature or with art, music or the sounds of silence in our prayer, in friendship or alone, we are awakened to a larger dimension to life. For a moment in time it can feel as if there are no missing pieces.

I can grow by sending my roots down into the deepest part of my being. Or I can be a slave to the wheel of labor, but is this the handiwork I give to God?

9.   *Deepest Longings*

Our deepest longings are operative in our relationships, through our ingestions, and through our possessions. In all these things we seek a fulfillment which is not theirs to give. We look to a certain relationship to complete our existence, or we try to smooth over our rough edges by eating or drinking excessively or habitually; or we turn to our electronics for immediate release of tension. We experience a hunger, we seek a fulfillment in what we can see, taste and touch. Behind our sense of hunger is a deeper and more authentic yearning that was planted in us at birth; it is a longing for God. The key word is displacement, and we seek gratification in our immediate surroundings, even as it eludes us.

In the process we give ourselves away in slavery to that which is not God. The focus in life becomes this lesser god. There is fear, not freedom. In freedom we choose. In fear we attach and we desire to control, just as we experience being controlled. A lesser god means a lesser self, because we cannot grow past our god. Only a more powerful love, greater than any love that we can see, taste and touch can invite us to move from our attachments and addictions.

When it seems as if we have nothing, because eventually we find that our lesser god cannot sustain us, we discover an invitation to a deeper love; it is the love which has brought us to our other loves in the first place. The presence of such a love creates in us an opening and a softening, and there begins the healing process. There comes a softening of the heart, and in the softening we are given access to contentment and joy. We begin to see past our attachments. We begin to experience the joy that does not tarnish. An opening has been created in us, and in the opening, in our woundedness, we are healed.

It is a long and winding road that takes us back to the one who has already found us. The spiritual truth, which becomes apparent in time, is that we are neither lost nor alone, and it is God's love that brings us back home. Our part is to consent, and to return love to Love eternal. We begin to feel at home, while still on the way.

10. *Wildflowers*

A little violet pushes her way up out of a crack in the concrete at the back porch: is this our domesticated city version of the wildflower? If we drive about an hour or two away from the city, when the season is right, we can see wildflower fields of poppies, lupine and larkspur. Against all odds, whether it be drought, wind and fire, or a concrete block of stone, each little flower follows with sensitivity the demands of the season. The wildflower has no intentional way of adjusting herself; she expresses herself just as she is. She has learned in whatever circumstances to be content. She blooms where she is planted, and she tends to bow to the sun. To the wildflower, where she is, is holy ground.

We follow the cycle of the little flower, and we see all of life reflected back to us. Just as we have experienced the time of the concrete block in our life, we can also recall our own circumstances of surviving periods of personal drought, the fires of conflict and tension, and knowing the need for air and greater space. In God's time we come to complete dependence on the light, and the need to be rooted somewhere. For us to see into her true nature, to experience the firmament, maybe we need to take off our shoes, for where we stand is holy ground (Exodus 3:5). When we are deeply rooted in the love of Christ it is possible to find within us the necessary strength when we are met with opposing forces.

Opposing forces come from natural elements and from persons who have motives, plans and affections quite different from our own. Sometimes it can seem like a very long time that we remain in a relationship or in a situation, doubting, wondering, and not knowing who we are in it. Remaining in a relationship over the long haul is a little like contemplative prayer: it can seem like a very long time passes with nothing happening. Relationships hold a very large element of mystery, and few of life's questions are answerable. We wait for blossoms and fruits. When the fruits come, we are granted the grace of recognition.

Sometimes when we think about the power of little things like the wildflower, it can seem like there are no little things. Like the wildflower, we bow to the Son.

11. *Heartbeat of the Parish*

The word community refers to a way of being together that gives us a sense of belonging. Often we complain that we do not experience much community, and we wonder how we can create a better one; or we experience a crisis or a benevolence, and wonder how we would ever get along without one.

Although we can say many things about Christian community, the one thing that is always true is that the Christian community is a waiting one. There is hardly any such thing as good, better or best. It is just exactly what it is, nothing more, nothing less than what it is: waiting. It is always as if something is missing, because it is. And we are based in need. We feel the need for a sense of community; otherwise we would not be here at all. We live and wait in faith for the complete fulfillment.

It is not without reason that the Church is called a pilgrim church forever in process, moving toward a goal as yet unattained. In *The God Who Comes*, Carlo Caretto writes about this larger picture of church: "How baffling you are, oh Church, and yet how I love you! You have made me suffer, and yet how much I owe you! I should like to see you destroyed, and yet I need your presence. You have given me so much scandal, and yet you have made me understand sanctity. I have seen nothing in the world more devoted to obscurity, more compromised, more false, and I have touched nothing more pure, more generous, more beautiful... I cannot free myself from you, because I am you, although not completely." Holy baffle! I am church. I am, with you, and you with me, one bread, one body.

Just as we are each a person in process, and so not finished yet, so also it is with community. Each community is a community in process, in transition toward a greater goal. If I doubt that God can work through all the struggles within my own parish, then by my own definition I am putting limits on God's grace.

Ours is a way toward perfection. We have not yet attained the goal. Discouragement and restlessness, individually and in community are God's way of calling us to a deeper faith and trust. There is the occasional glimpse of (aha!) insight when divine reality prevails over human frailty, and we are given a marker toward which we strive to attain the goal, together in faith. Out of this pinhole vision of light, we perceive a sense of direction. From whatever our individual experience is each one of us bears some measure of responsibility for becoming a connecting link, that the heartbeat be not one of isolation but one that is the collective heart, the heartbeat of the parish.

12. *Preferring Christ*

God has ordered balance and harmony. The silent and majestic wonder of the love of God is present in every aspect of the created world. God has created all creatures to be interdependent, and through faith we are given access to the joy that does not tarnish. We need to listen for what our part is in it, because there is something that is larger and more powerful than our instinctual and involuntary weaknesses.

No matter where on earth we happen to be, we are called in hundreds of ways each day to make decisions out of preference for Christ. We are called to put Christ before every decision, whether it be with regard to the quality and quantity of our ingestions, our relationships that we might be freed in love, our work (am I really destined to do this the rest of my life?), our leisure (what leisure?), or for the environment (God forgive us, we are only beginning to know what we do). Life is more complicated than it was 2000 years ago. We know more, and in the process, we know less.

St. Paul's reflections on how easily we fall into our weaknesses and out of alignment with God's design are included in a letter to the church in Rome (Romans 7:14-25). He observes his inability to understand his own behavior, his failure to carry out the things he wanted to do, and his doing instead the very things he didn't want to do. We not only travel the same road with one another, but we have also the assurance of St. Paul that it is not easy. We wobble in our spirituality. We wobble off our center over into being centered in our problems and our weaknesses, and we become centered in them instead of in Christ.

We are each a person in process, and we are called to a very special kind of listening, a listening with our hearts. Our lives are filled with many voices competing for our attention. Listening comes to us in the quiet, with time daily for personal prayer and reflection. Samuel heard God calling in the night (Samuel 3:1-18), God came to Jacob in a dream (Genesis 32:11), and Jesus went to the desert to pray (Luke 5:16). God comes to us today in our hearts, but this is not likely the loudest voice we will hear.

We are deeply challenged to not only live serenely, but to make concrete decisions out of the place where prayer and action meet. We are drawn together into the community of believers to be for one another what is too difficult to be individually, out of preference for Christ.

ALONG THE WAY

1. Along the Way
2. Changes in the Landscape
3. Generations of Travelers
4. Courtesy of Heart
5. Letting You Know Me
6. Between Two Points
7. Vessels of Blessedness
8. God's Tender Mercy
9. Beyond Our Reticence
10. Completing the Picture
11. Spiritual Generosity
12. Splendors of the Firmament

Then they told what had happened on the road, and how he had been made known to them in the breaking of the bread.
– Luke 24:35

1.   Along the Way

There were two who traveled together down the dry and dusty road toward a distant village. Along the way they talked about all the things that had happened in recent days. They were confused, felt abandoned and were depressed. They were joined by a third person who asked them why they were sad. In dismay they responded with a question: "Are you the only stranger in Jerusalem who does not know the things that have taken place there in these days?" (Luke 24:18). The stranger became a traveling companion, and walked with them.

At the close of the day the two invited the stranger to share a meal. The stranger took the bread, blessed it, broke it, and shared it with them. In the breaking of the bread their eyes were opened and they knew him. In the knowing, he vanished from their sight. They left that very hour to go back to Jerusalem to share the good news with their brothers and sisters in faith. They told about the things that had happened out on the road, and how he was made known to them in the breaking of the bread (Luke 24:13-35).

At the outset the two who traveled together shared a grief: the one who they hoped had come as their savior was gone. He promised them eternal life and yet he was gone. In their despair, confusion and desolation they could not see until they were given a sign. And yet out of their own spiritual hunger they were able to extend to the stranger. It seems their faith was working when they did not know it.

Our feet walk that same road. In spiritual friendship and out of preference for community we choose to walk the way together. We too have experienced despair in our lives. We have known broken dreams, brokenness in relationships, doubt, tension, tears and the need to let go. We've been in need of blessed assurance and reminders of immortality. The two along the way saw and heard the good news. Their perceptions were altered in the light of spiritual truth. Their hearts were filled, and the journey was made clearer.

For us today, invitation and opportunity remain the same, and every once in a while we are privileged to see a piece of spiritual truth as we continue along the way, breaking the bread of our lives with one another.

2. *Changes in the Landscape*

The road for them over 2000 years ago at times seemed barren. There were experiences of spiritual drought and periods of unknowing. Like them we are seekers on a journey.

When we speak of going on a journey there is a sense of movement implied. We travel from one place to another and our perceptions are altered. There are changes in the landscape if we travel by foot or by car. If we travel by ship there are changes in the seascape. The sea becomes a reflection of every human temperament known to us, ranging from peaceful and reflective to tempestuous. If we travel by plane there is rapid and radical change in our perspective of earth and sky. The early travelers knew only changes of land and sea, but there is change of a deeper nature we share with all generations, and that is change in the soulscape we experience in response to God's call.

Change is a naturally occurring phenomenon. Human attachments, attitudes and behaviors can block what would happen naturally. Whether we journey by land, sea or sky or we embark on a journey of the soul, there are three parts to it: the part we have left, the part where we are, and the part where we will be. We can only be in one place at a time.

For the journey of the soul, we need to leave behind all that is excess baggage in the eyes of God. We carry excesses in our hearts and in our hands. We need to leave behind all but the thin spiritual line that connects us to God and to one another. The journey of the soul requires strength, trust and courage for what we cannot see and do not know. It becomes clear that faith and courage travel hand in hand, or we do not travel at all.

The spiritual winds of change come from many different directions. God speaks to the unfettered heart, and the heart in this condition hears no other voice. From the perspective of the inner landscape of the soul, if we stop to reflect on our soul journey to date any geographical changes would seem pale compared with changes of the interior that we have experienced along the spiritual pathway.

Following periods of spiritual hunger and darkness, it is often made clear that God's will has been made manifest in our life when we were neither seeking nor directly aware. In God's time, there comes a single, well-ordered vision and a sense of direction for the next phase of the journey. From the many directions there comes one: I am where I am by the grace of God.

3. Generations of Travelers

The two who traveled together on the road to Emmaus carried a sense of community along with their feelings of consolation in light of the assurance of the resurrection. When their perceptions were altered, they knew the story needed to be shared back with their community.

Since then, times have become increasingly complex. Once we were generations sharing common ground, with the support of community to share the joys and to ease us through times of transition. Times are different today. Through the centuries, the meaning of community has taken on new form. We say we feel it disappearing. We yearn for its presence when we experience life changing before our very eyes. We wish to share the good news face to face. We are often left wondering how it is that the story moves from personal insight to shared vision, wisdom and faith.

Within the cycle of change, we see that the land we might have once inherited as our base in an agrarian culture may now cost us many times what our fathers earned in a lifetime. Families are likely to be geographically scattered, and traditional family units sometimes become stepping units to new lives. Friends acquired along the way may be gone within the year to seek new opportunities elsewhere. New construction goes up and we forget what was there. We erase ourselves. Ritual and tradition slip away. We experience discontinuity in family relationships and community life, and it can seem as if the traditional anchors for the sense of self no longer exist. We raise the questions of a new generation, seeking ways to solidarity and unification.

Every generation feels that change comes especially to them. Change comes to all generations, and it is always seen and understood best in retrospect. The challenge is to come to new ground within the light of our faith. Our hearts may find rest in the awareness that every day holds fresh invitation and opportunity to partake of the consolation. Opportunity comes in the form of breaking and sharing the bread of our life with one another with an attitude of humility, gentleness, and courtesy of heart. Our coming together becomes a celebration of a mystical unity already in place: for a moment in time, as well as for all of time, we are partakers of the consolation. Precious anchors can be found in the moment.

4. Courtesy of Heart

There is a little story of St. Francis of Assisi, who when wandering with his friends through the countryside stooped to pick up a yellow daisy from the edge of the road. As he was putting out his hand, he suddenly restrained himself. He changed his mind: perhaps the Lord had sent the little flower to adorn the road. Maybe it is true that God has a better plan than mine for the flower. In his response to God's design, St. Francis chose to bend his knee to natural creation. Humility is a bend in the knee before all of nature and all of humanity. We notice it in one another as a certain reverence and courtesy of heart for what already exists.

Courtesy of heart seeks to affirm another in his or her process, with no particular attachment to outcomes. Results are in God's hands. To give encouragement and affirmation lies closer to spiritual truth than a compliment or flattery, which may be only a vain attempt to move things in a way that will help us to work together better, perhaps going in my direction. It is only from a base of not knowing or accepting myself that I will want to exercise control over the designs along the road of life.

The gift of affirmation is a grace, freely given, and seeks to meet another person where we are: together in the presence of God's grace. In contentment and reverence, there is no need to draw conclusions or make judgments about another. All of human life is respected in a moment, and valued aside from expectations. There is a sense of self-acceptance that extends to an acceptance of all circumstances.

When forgiveness in a relationship seems slow in coming, there comes a time when in the pain of waiting, we need to look a little more deeply inside for what the issues really are. The deeper issue can be different from the original incident that seemed to generate conflict in a relationship. The deeper issue can be one of humility. Just as St. Francis humbled himself before the flower, and Jesus humbled himself before all of human nature even to death, we follow in their ways when we can bend to another. Bending is a matter of integrity, reverence, and courtesy of heart. In reverence for all of God's creation, I free you to do God's will for you, and God may have a better plan for you than one of my own design.

5. *Letting You Know Me*

Ours is a relational theology. Some relationships are more fruitful than others. At times we can clearly see why, and at other times we feel baffled and in pain when a relationship feels closed. Every relationship involves an element of risk and very often the level of risk is directly related to our willingness to let another know us. Instead of letting you know who I am, we often focus on the other, getting inside another's thoughts, wondering about his or her feelings and behavior. To complete the relationship, to carry it to fruition, I need to let you know me. If I am a stranger to myself, then I am a stranger to you also. As deeply as I can begin to look at myself, so deeply can I begin to be with you, to begin to let you know who I am from my heart.

In letting you know me, I need to look at what blocks there may be to prevent that from happening. We all have certain issues of avoidance, and the blocks often come from them. Some of our avoidances may be rooted in conflict, anger, failure, pain or emptiness. Because it's hard for me to put my finger on something that I am avoiding, avoidances often sit as phantom blocks in a relationship. They will subdue the relationship, hold it back and even cause it to disintegrate until we can see into them enough to name them and call them our own. In God's time, we come to a fuller acceptance of our own limitations as well as our strengths. When we can become aware of how this happens in us, an opening is created for our ground of awareness to be transformed.

There are times when we are with another, and we know that we have been met and we are known. One sign of our knowing is that we feel freed of the fatigue of effort. When these kinds of meetings happen, both persons experience it. Defenses are dropped. There is an opening rather than guardedness. It is in the opening where we become conscious of the presence of the Holy Spirit. The Holy Spirit brings the freedom of God's grace. In the freedom of grace, our walk with God and with one another requires less effort. We walk in the light of Christ. It is in the enlightened relationship that the fruits will be made abundantly clear. It is here where we return time and time again. We return and remain, because we've been given precious bread for the journey.

6. Between Two Points

We all travel as exiles and pilgrims in this life, with a vision and a deeper longing for the homeland beyond the one that we already know. Just as our church is a pilgrim church, a community in progress in transition toward a greater goal, we too are pilgrims forever on a journey. If we are satisfied with our present condition, if we are comfortable with the present state of our soul or the state of the world, then we are not ready for the spiritual journey. Our restlessness and our readiness often coincide.

Our restlessness creates an inner tension between two points: our human will and God's will for us. The creative tension in the space between two points becomes the energy filled place where we are awakened to a larger dimension of life. This is the place where transformation happens. There is an ancient Latin phrase *per aspera ad astra*, "through the rough roads to the stars." The difficulties in life, the dark and rough places in the road, frequently precede spiritual transformation and healing.

We can see that the reality of the human condition does not change too much through the centuries. We are all more alike than we are different. We remain concerned for our basic nourishment, and for our physical safety. We wrestle against our weaknesses. We long for sustained peace and joy in our relationships. We seek the higher road of enlightenment and we believe God longs to bring us through the rough roads to a better place. It is in the light of God's love that the pathway is made smooth. Once our heart has become pierced by the love of God, love is clearly seen as the driving force of all good, made manifest in all of creation. Love is always an evening out, a smoothing out, is always spacious and never crowded.

Sometimes we are open to newness and transformation in others and miss seeing it in ourselves. Transformation really needs to be celebrated on all fronts as signs of God's intervening love. Once in a place of spiritual transformation, we find the dominant mood is one of joy and openness. Central to our line of vision is the mystery of God's love. Along the way of life, our vision becomes clearer and more direct, without shadows. Our human will gradually becomes more at one with God's will, granting us the grace of clarity and ease from tension. Newcomers are always welcome here!

7.   *Vessels of Blessedness*

The visionary is one who sees with fresh eyes beyond the immediacy of the moment. Children have this way about them, a way of seeing freely into the world of imagination, vision and contemplation, and of becoming present to circumstances beyond the obvious. The spiritual line of vision for a child can lead directly to a special awareness of a lighter, quieter and more reflective side to life. Jesus invites us to be like them.

Life is a mysterious and paradoxical mix of the sad and joyful, the empty and the full. In the process of understanding one's personal history, it may be necessary for a time to examine another side to life, the darker side, in order to release it to its own freedom. However if we look back over our earlier years and see only darkness and emptiness, then we may not be seeing the complete picture. Nothing exists without its opposite. Even while living within an outer dwelling of hindrance and distraction, a child may inwardly experience a spiritually balancing tendency toward natural contemplation. There comes an awareness of the ground that is holy. These may be called moments of blessedness.

Moments of blessedness most often occur in quiet, from out of the positive side of spiritual emptiness. They very often correspond to nature, and may extend just beyond the daydream into holy ground. A child has a particular way of seeing the clouds against the sky, the wind moving over a field of grass, or the moon shining on the water. With this vision there may come a sense of nurture, consolation and oneness. It is within the temporal emptiness of childlike surrender that space is created for the fullness of God's grace to enter in. Very often, it is in the empty spaces where the Holy Spirit is free to live and move and breathe.

In retrospect, in later years such moments of blessedness can be seen as signs of God's grace longing to touch us and make us whole, whether in the emptiness of our perceived aloneness or in the fullness of quietude. It can be a worthy challenge to glance backwards in time, scanning the spiritual horizons of one's early years, to find some of these special moments of blessedness to see more clearly, even in retrospect, God's unfailing love for us. God's love longs to touch us and heal us. We are reminded that somewhere along the way we have become vessels of blessedness with the fullness of Christ.

8.   *God's Tender Mercy*

The will of God is confirmed for us through many signs made visible today and for all of time. We see these signs in the breaking of the bread, in the promise of eternal life, and in the dawn of each new day. We see the signs also in our feelings that bring all of these things to new life. Our feelings come from an inward awareness of God's love. Tears are one of the signs of God's love for us.

Tears are not always of grief and sadness. The sunshine on the water can bring them too. So can a rose, a line from a hymn, or a special moment in prayer. The waters of love have a way of changing our perceptions. There comes a sense of loving and being loved. Our tears give testimony to our love and to an even greater love than ours that is working in us. The love comes as a sign that there has been much clearing out of the distractions to life, that the day to day garden varieties of troubles have been released by us to a greater good. It can almost seem as if the soul is working its way backwards to an original clarity once held before taking on all the complications of life. Life for a moment can seem simplified and unified. There is an element of tenderness and mercy. Our tears become our experience of God's tender mercy.

Tears of grief and sadness eventually through time lead to joy. Tears of God's tender mercy have already. Jesus likened the Holy Spirit to living water. There are many ways in which this living water comes to us in refreshment, washing all things new and clear. It is the nature of water to seek the lowest place to fill. It is the nature of tears of grace to come from the deepest place in the soul. From tears of this deeper more sensitive nature, we can perceive a sense of direction for where God would have us go. This is one way in which spiritual direction comes to us. It's as if God is asking us to wait, pause here for a little while; the lessons are deep and rich, and could be missed if we pass by too quickly.

In experiencing God's tender mercy in the gift of tears, we become the bearer of an inner revelation. With the experience comes a softening of the heart. We are reminded that those who walked the road to Emmaus experienced a joy that exceeded their sorrow.

9. *Beyond Our Reticence*

The birth of every new venture along the way presupposes some sense of disorganization. Toward each new experience we carry with us random interferences and disorganized trivia, some of which may or may not be relevant. Our reference frames can feel clouded. Sometimes in looking toward the future I can experience all my insecurities of yesterday. We reach for some piece of knowledge, seeking security, and we can only reach back into our past because no knowledge outside of our faith exists for the future. We are stepping into the unknown. In times of personal transition, a feeling of holding back may prevail. We look at a new relationship, or a new piece of work, or a new geography and we become tentative and reticent in the face of what could be perceived as invitation and opportunity.

Our source of fear or reticence can be external or internal. Internal fear is what we carry within us and can be related to previous experiences and self-doubt. Fear can be external, and related to practical physical or emotional safety concerns. Some fear can give us a proper sense of caution. We look to the example of our risen Lord and Savior. The way of Jesus is to give up one's life, carrying only reminders of what I have with me in this moment as being sufficient in the light of my faith (Matthew 16:25).

In the challenges that come to us, we move in two spheres: the temporal and the spiritual. We compete in one. Sometimes our fears are based in comparing ourselves with what others do and how well they appear to be doing it. This would be a wrong route for our creativity. Our spiritual nature would have us free in thought from any earthly attachments to outcomes and the opinions of others. Our source of creative inspiration is in God, and God who inspires us will see us through.

Everyone needs an advocate. We have been given one in the Holy Spirit. This is the voice that merits listening. In prayerful moments of wholeness and oneness we can experience convergence of inspiration and insight with a glimpse of a foundation for action. The two spheres become one. It is as if for a time I stand at the center of a celestial body where there are no shadows and all sides of the light can be seen. The light stands synonymous with the love of God, and the love of God serves to displace my fears. In such times we are invited to move beyond our reticence, out of the present and toward the unknown, because fear is the place beyond which I will not grow unless I stretch myself.

10. *Completing the Picture*

Our line of vision takes on a certain field of movement at any given time. Often our field of movement, or our field of reality is defined in terms of the work at hand, and then translated by our mood of the moment. With our limited line of vision, sometimes we can neither see around nor through the complications that are most evident. It can seem as if life is a continual matter of the squeaky wheel getting the oil with the negativity clamoring the loudest for our attention and getting it all. Living the distractions becomes the center of our life. We can actually feel ourselves wobbling off our spiritual center over into being centered in the distraction. This is human nature. We are affected. It is with only a shift in perception that I can actually take myself out of external influences and return to my true center in God.

A visionary is one who knows that every picture has 360 degrees, and remembers that there is always a picture beyond the one we are seeing. We do not avoid distractions and problems in this life. However when we become centered in them, we have allowed our external situation to take us from the effectiveness of God's love. We live, breathe, sleep (or don't sleep) and eat (or don't eat) the problem; or we drink it. It can seem as if the problem or conflict becomes our whole life. But in the balancing light of spiritual truth, the problem is only a piece of our life.

As aware as we all are of the tensions and conflict points in our lives it is important that we not miss the complete picture from the contemplative perspective, one that includes the lighter and quieter side to life. This is our spirituality. Once we begin to see the complete picture, we actually experience a different felt sense in our body. That different sense won't make a lot of noise, and so we have to become quieted to hear it.

We have within us a spiritually balancing tendency toward wholeness. We can remain fully aware of our difficulties but we are centered in God. When we feel centered in God, we can experience the subtle movement from desolation to consolation. Consolation takes on many forms. The common denominator would be inner peace. Peace creates space for joy. Joy creates balance for our fear and anxiety. In completing the picture, we can begin to know the freedom to see life in the balancing light and love of spiritual truth.

11. Spiritual Generosity

Jesus came sent by God, walked with us for a little while teaching us the way we should go, then gave his life for us. God sent the Holy Spirit, the Paraclete, our helper to bring balance, harmony and vitality into all of creation, weaving all things to one. Three become One, for us.

Jesus, sent by God, knows all of our needs. Our essential needs include water and food. Jesus came to promise us the living waters of heaven, and the bread of life. Jesus taught us to love God and our neighbor. My neighbor is the one with whom I stand face to face in any given moment. In the specific way that I find this hard, here I have identified the way in which God wants me to grow. Spiritual generosity is giving without motive or attachment to outcome; it is giving because an opportunity has been presented.

Jesus is our earthly benchmark for spiritual generosity. Jesus came to bear witness to good, the good that is the love of God. Jesus came to teach us in the way we should go, the way of goodness. Jesus did not just come to teach goodness to the good; Jesus came to teach the one who would listen. Jesus kept company with the ones who would pause in their lives to listen to him. Those with whom Jesus walked were often outside the boundaries of goodness as determined by the establishment. In the teachings of Jesus, no one is excluded for any reason we could witness or imagine.

In every moment of our life, we stand at a doorway anticipating entry, trusting in God to guide our "yes." The doorway to spiritual generosity was opened for each one of us at our conception, and the invitation to remain is unceasing. In the Body of Christ, there is no "I, me or mine." We are given a spiritual nature of empathy and compassion. The gifts of God multiply by giving them away. There is no ownership. By contrast, in the material world, if I am given a car and I give the car to you, I am minus a car. In spiritual giving I am not minus anything. I am given love and I give love to you. Love is magnified, and multiplied. A spiritual gift received, then shared, is twice given, twice kept: this is the spark and tinder of God's mystical arithmetic.

12. *Splendors of the Firmament*

When the heavens are seen from here, one can feel very small. For us here below, God has given us a path to follow. God sent Jesus to take away our distance from God and to guide our feet along the perilous pathways of life. With the light of Christ we feel less inclined to yield to the shadows. Little moments of grace begin very gradually to build upon themselves in the soul forming clusters resembling a microcosm of the celestial beings: I am magnificent-ly formed in God's image and God is all. What sweet surrender to acknowledge my nothingness before God's everythingness. We are the people of God's grand canvass of earth and sky, and what artistry we do see.

With our star rising out of the east, the configuration of the splendors of the firmament became irrevocably changed. God does not leave us orphaned. God does not send us pain. Pain comes from sources other than God. When we find ourselves in painful situations, God will weep when we weep. God will stand with us in the center of our pain and guide us through to a better way. The splendors of the firmament are fixed high above the earth. Unlike them, we are grounded, mutable and ever hopeful of change for the better. We see quite a magnificent cluster of heavenly bodies reflected here below in the human heart when we can return to our original clarity that existed before we took on so many things in life. In the splendors of the firmament, we see perfection formed in the image of God, and shaped by the hand of God.

God has given us the ground of prayer found beneath our feet, and the sky above as well. The firmament reflects the constancy of the lasting promises of God. When scanning the darkness of the skies we can see quite a magnificent cluster of celestial bodies. With our limited perspective, we can see only one side of a celestial body. We can only partially comprehend. Even so: how mysteriously magnificent.

ORDER YOUR DAYS

1.   Our Mystical Roots
2.   Our Mystical Roots and the Surface Tensions
3.   Ease of Exit
4.   The Unfettered Journey
5.   Befriend the Darkness
6.   Individuality, Creativity and Paradox
7.   Confessing My Powerlessness
8.   The Contemplative Heart

I have loved you with an everlasting love. – Jeremiah 31:3

1.   *Our Mystical Roots*

Prayer is larger than we are. When we pray we join in a steady stream of prayer that is over 2000 years old. Out of that ancient place of grace there is a voice of deep strength calling us inward and away from the voices of external influences that bring disorganization and disorder to our days.

With the world around us in a constant state of chaotic flux, there is a special grace in knowing there is a place that is sacred and unchanging, a place where we can go to be renewed in the love that is ours by way of grace. The effect of God's grace is to bring us back to our original and intended course, with a yearning for increased holiness and infinite goodness.

It can seem like a very long and winding way back to the one who formed us so long ago. In truth the journey to God is short and direct because the love that God has for us has brought God very near, even closer than my hand is to my face. In our prayer today we touch the common source and the strength of our Christian heritage, the mystical roots of God's grace.

Within any system there are beginnings and middles and ends of cycles, even as the roots remain constant and stable, continuous through time. An organism cannot live too far from its roots. Putting down roots, knowing our roots, touching our roots benefits us as it does the tree. Trees receive water through their roots. Leaves grow toward the light. Roots grow toward water, and hold the plant in the ground. The roots serve to stabilize the tree, giving it belonging in the ground. The tree bears fruit in due season. The tree cannot ignore the life source of its roots.

For the body of the Church, just as with the tree, our strength is in our roots. Traces of the mystical roots of the church show up in the writings of the saints and mystics of the church; they show up also in the feats of monumental construction of the Gothic churches and cathedrals of Europe. There is no one who can remain unaffected by entering through their doors and spending a few moments in quiet wonder. Those monuments stand today as a testimony to our strength against time.

In the complexity of our modern times, when we see new construction go up sometimes we forget what was there. It can feel as if our past is so quickly erased it no longer applies. It does.

2. Our Mystical Roots and the Surface Tensions

Our belonging is rooted in our past, and in an even deeper past before us. Through the writings of the saints and mystics of the church, we have been shown the ground of the fullness of life immersed in a sea of pain, as well as life fully grounded in the Love of God. The same ancient truths remain for us today: God's grace is present, silent and unseen, deep and strong. We can return to the mystical roots of our existence to order our days, or we can draw disorder from the complex external influences of today. The choice is always ours.

Every system and organism has roots in its source of origin, or it ceases to exist. We walk the weary road of life with an awareness of the inevitable faults, cracks and surface tensions of all of our human systems, secular and sacred. Tensions bring change and eventually yield to release and rest. The visible and influential stresses found in the church today need to be seen as they are: painfully real and transitory distractions and weaknesses. When we become singularly caught up in the currents of the surface tensions, the truth of the negativity becomes louder than the truth of the positive. We become like the tree that draws life too far from its roots.

The faults and tensions that activate our feelings need not be diminished; it is also true that they are not our essential life source. The part of the tree that is visible can go through periods of wind, fire and drought and yet survive when the roots are established. With surface changes, the roots remain faithfully in place holding all within the system very dear to the earth.

Together we bear the load of life, with God at the center. Because we are One Body, and given the nature of the church, we need to go outside ourselves, but not without first going inside to recover what feels momentarily lost: our original oneness in the ground of the mystical roots of God's grace. We have been granted the capacity to draw deeply from the well of the living waters of our faith. The organism will endure in response to new challenges when the root system remains strong and deep, even when the surface tensions leave visible signs of stresses. The mystical roots of the church continue to be an ancient and continuous source of strength for us today, and silently they are so beautiful. What a time it is for us to be present!

3. *Ease of Exit*

The spiritual journey is an unending one to eternal life. Along the way we have need of a resting place. Our resting place is in God. Our rest is God's delight. God's delight is our blessing. When we let our hearts rest in nature, or with art or music, or with the sound of silent prayer with another or alone, we are awakened to a new dimension of life. For a moment in time, it can feel as if there are no missing pieces.

Even so, as well intended as we may be, in the course of every day there are many things that can take us sideways or backwards. The technology of human communications is irrevocably and radically changed. Life has become complex and quick, and becomes out of balance when the primary influences are technical, external and unceasing. We live interruptive lives far from our original intended nature filled with grace.

In all of our systems, both sacred and secular, we have instant and unfiltered communication. Just as quickly as I am connected, I can disconnect. If I no longer favor the way communication is going, I can press quit or delete or exit, and feel immediately relieved for having done so. If I am dissatisfied with my work, my relationships, or my church I can delete that too. We can find ourselves wandering in a contemporary urban wilderness unable to spot what is missing.

Restlessness becomes the exit point based on one's experience that life does not appear to be working in the given moment. The paradox is that restlessness in relationships, in community and in prayer may be a sign that a person is clearly on the brink of a deeper spirituality. I may feel confusion, as if I have lost my faith when indeed, I have grown out of the faith that once was mine. God may be guiding me to a deeper avenue of faith. I can take a step to correct the course of my interruptive life when I can delete some of the external voices, and when I can press pause for a moment of recollection.

All of our systems are characterized by ease of exit, but God does not want us to be short changed. God pulled the Israelites out of the fray of life and spoke to them in the wilderness. Is this a time to pause and to seek our own spiritual wilderness? Is this a time to know in a deeper way the meaning of contemplation? Is this a time to find an hour of quiet, or to schedule a day or two of silence in a monastic retreat? Life has gaps. The Israelites had already wandered in the desert for 40 years in search of the Promised Land. Do I need to wait so long?

4.   The Unfettered Journey

We experience life at two levels: the obvious and the sacred. Eventually they become one because everything does. When we are grounded in the obvious we become like the tree that has over-extended growth at the top, and stands in need of pruning. There is in each of us a sacred knowing of what is too much and what is enough.

God has created an order, balance and harmony to our existence and our first job is to listen attentively for what is our part. We can ask: who am I without all that I see, hear, touch and possess? In my irreducible minimum, I am God's. Sometimes it can seem like we spend the first half of life enriching our existence by taking life on, then we can spend the second half casting off our excesses in order to return to the truth that is central to our existence: I am loved and called precious in God's sight.

Jesus says: "Come to me, all you that are weary, and I will give you rest" (Matthew 11:28). Jesus did not say pack it all up, and bring it all with you. We are hunters and gatherers, but Jesus said not for this mission. Jesus said try coming empty handed. It's possible to feel empty, and yet full of the demands of the people, places and things we encounter through the course of our day. It's possible to feel isolated in a day filled with people. The day feels out of balance; we carry the load of life, we are tired. But wait, am I full, or am I fulfilled?

There is a big difference between filled and fulfilled, just as there is a big difference between feeling empty and the emptiness of the unfettered heart in contemplative prayer to our God who loves us through each day. The groundwork of life requires prioritized attentiveness. In contemplative prayer we come to God empty handed and open hearted, aware of our need for grace. God speaks to the unfettered heart, and in this moment the heart hears no other voice. For a moment in time, the sacred and the obvious are one. I am neither ahead nor behind; I am where I can be.

5. *Befriend the Darkness*

We seek constancy in the spiritual journey; we encounter restlessness, doubt and despair. Sometimes our days feel long and dark. We wonder how on earth to find that lovely leveling off place of grace, and there remain.

When I am in a place of darkness my first inclination is toward action. Thoughts race through my mind: this is my ground. Oh no: wait, this isn't my ground. Where then is my ground? I need to find my ground. When I am not grounded in good, my first inclination is often toward active avoidance and involves other people, places and things. I falsely believe my actions will lift me from out of the darkness. I feel inclined to shop, eat, move, change jobs or relationships, or I go to my electronics. All this translates to action. The opposite is what is needed.

Ours is a God of tenderness. Spiritual darkness can be creatively productive when we do not break faithfulness. When we break faithfulness, we pacify the darkness by turning actively to our senses for release from tension. In contrast, we can do surprisingly well when we sign on for it. When we remain in a situation or in a relationship over the long haul, we bear witness to the fact that God needs time to guide us through to a better way, and that Love is stronger than wrong.

God is here for us, now. We listen for the silent voices, and for the disparaging voices; they may be received as a sign to go deeper into myself. If I find one voice of affirmation, I take it silently into account. If I find two voices, I take them silently into account. Given a fair measure of psychological stability, continue to go deeper. Our darkness creates an empty space into which the Holy Spirit can live and move and breathe. We pray to be open to God in the emptiness of our silence. What we find within us: we are letting God be God.

In our perceived emptiness, the vessel of our soul receives the blessing of God. The tree stands open and empty against the dark days of winter. The leaves have fallen away. In the emptiness the rain continues to strengthen the roots, keeping faithfulness for the new leaves that will come when the rhythm of the sun is right. On all things, love waits. It is not too long to wait on love. In our waiting, we are granted the grace to touch the sacred wounds of the Body of Christ.

6.   *Individuality, Creativity and Paradox*

The creative spirit is one of originality and expressiveness of thought, has no spare parts and sees with the eyes of a child, with no excess baggage. The creative spirit soars when it is given free reign in the ground of God. The creative thinker is the one who will make changes, beginning from within, will not be tempted by conformity, and will believe without question in the potential for new life.

In our early history, the desert fathers gave new life and vitality to the whole church returning by way of prayer to the mystical roots of the Body of Christ. They became advocates of solitude, silence and prayer. Did the desert fathers refuse to passively accept the cultural disarray of their time? If so, then were they rebellious, or were they seekers of wisdom and truth? Or both? They certainly were not thinking like others; they were going against the grain of the times. Our contemplative roots can be traced to them.

In generalities, we can apply to our lives what we have learned from them: keep originality of thought, keep your thoughts faithful to your heart, and keep your heart grounded in God. In disturbance of thought, draw closer to God. Don't copy others: be the one others copy. Verify yourself in God, and not through the eyes of others. Beyond all understanding, God is at work in you changing your heart before you can change your mind. From this perspective, the desert father or mother, the hermit or the monk is countercultural and so are we when we make the choice to spend an hour in silent surrender to our God who loves us through each moment.

Those with whom Jesus walked were often outside the boundaries of goodness as determined by the establishment, that is the ruling body defined by conformity. We can be stretched by the tensions of conformity, or we can find our ultimate rest and release in contemplation of our God who brings new life. The choice remains ours.

At the close of the darkness of winter, all of our hope is hinged on the solitary green leaf beginning to appear in the earliest part of the season of spring. This is living proof that our strength is in our roots. Christian renewal came from out of the desert, and continues to come today in the hearts of all believers who are willing to expose the desert areas of the human heart to the living waters of the Love of God.

7.   *Confessing My Powerlessness*

The subject of contemplation is being introduced and widely promoted in the medical, educational, and corporate worlds under the concept of mindfulness, and has long been embraced in 12 step spirituality, where confessing my powerlessness is the initial step one takes toward spiritual awakening and transformation.

In various times and ways, each one of us has tapped into the disordered-ness and the unmanageability of life. When we continue to take on all that life brings to us, we can all too easily fall to the belief that our lives are too busy and that time goes by too quickly. We fall victim to our false self, and away from the truth: time never changes. The passage of time is the same now as it was for Moses. Time cannot be managed. What we can manage is what we put into the time we are given. Cultural stimuli seek to keep us filled to overflowing. We live our lives based in external influences, causing us to live interruptive lives far from our original intended nature filled with grace.

We can begin to wonder: what on earth is so commanding? Who is in command? The disciplined heart, which becomes the disciplined mind, has the capacity to turn inward, returning to the stable base of our spiritual foundations where peace and harmony are in command. Restlessness, invitation and opportunity remain today, just as was so for Moses. The pendulum of the clock swings far and wide, finding the center-point of perfect balance at regular intervals. We can do no less than the clock.

In contemplation, it's possible to find release from the fatigue of the tensions of effort and secular competition by confessing one's powerlessness and yielding to a strength that is greater than our own. We become quietly present in our open and undefended self in the presence of God. The transformative effect is to bring us back to our original and intended course with a yearning for increased holiness and infinite goodness, in the company of a power greater than our own, longing to heal us and make us whole.

8. *The Contemplative Heart*

When Moses saw the burning bush, he stopped to take off his shoes to stand on the ground that is holy (Exodus 3:5). The holiness of the ground remains. From the time of Moses we have been given the ground within that lessens the hold fear has on our human nature. We can touch the holy ground when we pause and venture into the silence and solitude of our heart. We are invited to take time to cast off our shoes and whatever else is coming before God in any given moment. In so doing, we recover what is beyond the senses.

There is a line, straight and thin, that transcends time and connects us to God and to one another. The thin spiritual line can be drawn between two fixed positions; it becomes indirect when weighted down by excesses carried in our hands and in our hearts. Jesus came to change hearts. When my heart is changed, my perceptions are changed. When my perceptions are changed, my behavior is changed. A small shift brings a new vision. God's grace is for keeps and is cumulative in us. When I sense an absence, one of us has walked away.

There has been no special place in history reserved for the prophets, saints and mystics of the church; they can be found in every generation and are as alive today as ever, beginning with the children. Jesus invites us to become like them: "Truly I tell you, unless you change and become like children, you will never enter the kingdom of heaven" (Matthew 18:3). Jesus calls us to new life, and wants us to feel at home with ease and familiarity. By being quietly attentive to God's presence we are granted the grace to see beyond the immediacy of the present moment. We begin to see what was unseen. From the contemplative perspective, the heart is not an effort driven organ but responds with easy and gentle gratitude to God's unfailing grace. Our way of life becomes one of contemplative recovery of all that is true and good, kind and gentle.

The contemplative heart towers above nothing, embraces all, loves God, loves neighbor and forgives all the rest. Our mystical roots spread far and wide through the generations. In all heavenly oneness, we are the roots, the leaves and the branches. We have been called by Jesus to remain under the drip line of the living waters sent down from heaven, trusting in God's overwhelming tenderness and infinite mercy showered upon us with every heartbeat, bearing faithful witness to the mystical fact of God's grace: God's kingdom comes.

I have loved you with an everlasting love. – Jeremiah 31:3

Section Three: Examination of Consciousness

"Come to me all you that are weary, and I will give you rest."
– Matthew 11:28

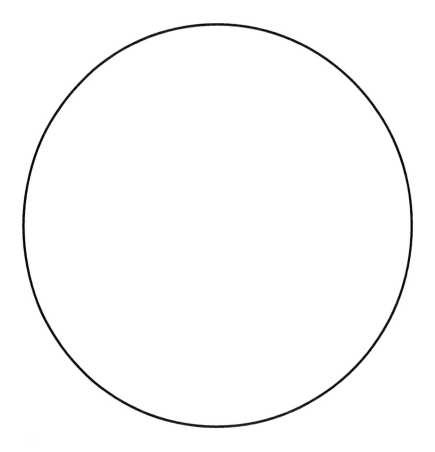

Wherever I am

There are worlds within worlds
within worlds
and there is a map

We are always at a doorway awaiting
anticipating entry
living not as an outsider
in my own life but central to every
entrance and exit, turning, turning saying
yes, I think so

EXAMINATION OF CONSCIOUSNESS

INTRODUCTION

Each of us longs for belonging and our basic search is what drives our lives. Life tends to give us incessant auditory and visual input; the sounds and the sights are compelling. We wonder: do we belong here, or do we belong there? Or where? Jesus says stop, don't go there, but "come unto me, and I will give you rest" (Matthew 11:28). Jesus invites us to come to him, to follow him, and to not bring too many things with us: no money, no bag for the journey, and no spare clothing, sandals, or walking staff (Luke 9:3). If acceptance is not found based on these simple principles, then Jesus says "shake the dust from your feet" (Matthew 10:14) and come where you belong. Jesus very clearly in simple terms defines belonging, invites us to him and shows us the way.

We seek to live ordered, disciplined lives. Through the course of each day there are many things that can take us sideways or backwards. Because the spiritual journey is one of continual change the contemporary spirit is invited, even compelled to live a life of perpetual examination of one's thoughts and actions.

The spiritual journey has three parts to it: the place where we were, the place where we are, and the place where we will be. We can only be in one place at one time. Jesus defines belonging and shows us the way: "If any want to become my followers, let them deny themselves and take up their cross daily and follow me" (Luke 9:23). We cannot take up the cross of Jesus if our hands are filled with too many people, places and things from the past or the present, or we are filled with worries about the future. In contemplative prayer we turn to God empty handed and open hearted, insofar as we are able, trusting in the spiritual generosity of God to give us what is needed for today.

For most of us the way our lives are set up, whether we have major or minor challenges, the problem is finding and maintaining our spiritual balance. Negativity is louder than the positive. In contrast God's grace comes to us in the quiet, often in the stillness of prayer. Transformation comes gradually. Over time we become more and more attentive to God's strong silent presence living in us. The stable ground within us, the bedrock of our faith, grows to become stronger than any of the external distractions and obstacles in life.

The bedrock of our faith is found in the ground of our prayer, the ground of God. Our Christian tradition has retained three major prayer expressions: vocal, meditative and contemplative. Jesus did not categorize prayer too much, and most of us feel inclined to pray in varieties of ways. Over time we are likely to develop a preference for a particular way of prayer, but not to the exclusion of another. The following exercises tend to focus on contemplative prayer, but not to the exclusion of vocal prayer or meditation.

As you become familiar with the flow of the exercises, you will notice that each examination period can be broken down into two parts. The first part (Reading Instructions) consists of designated readings for the week, followed by a period of silent contemplative prayer. For the second part (Examination Instructions) there is a slight shift in consciousness involving the circle meditation, with instructions for examination and meditation. Meditation may as well extend to vocal prayer, silent or spoken. Mediation on various aspects of our life can lead to clarification, and ultimately to the wordless gratitude of contemplation.

The contemplative perspective, once acquired, shapes our thinking, our attitudes and behavior. We gain much from observing our own lives as well as the lives of others as opposed to reacting or responding. Contemplative observation implies the ability to look at and reflect on what we see with feeling as well as thought, and with involvement as well as detachment. The freedom of choice remains ours. We do not seek to be perfect, but we do seek the refining influence of God's grace. Day by day we come to see more clearly the unfettered truth that is central to our existence: I am loved and called precious in God's sight.

The examination exercises are presented in six parts, with the suggestion that the exercises be done over a period of six weeks. However the exercises can be completed in one week, one day at a time, in an undistracted setting such as a retreat house or a monastic environment. Faithfulness, openness and dedication are more essential than the amount of time spent in each period. Thirty minutes daily is recommended; however if you offer five minutes that is perhaps five minutes more than was so yesterday. Regarding the structure of the format for the exercises, spiritual balance comes with the reader developing a circular rhythm of read, pray, examine, and then repeating the cycle with each new day.

There is an order applied to the rhythm of each week's lesson. The basic spiritual disciplines of prayer, fasting and almsgiving are kept in the following ways: for Weeks One and Two, we become grounded in our prayer with the intention to examine and observe our lives in a detached fashion, without attending to reforming them at this time. In Weeks Three and Four, we begin to see that there may be specific attitudes and behaviors from which we may choose to fast, or separate ourselves from in the process of being made new in Christ Jesus. In Weeks Five and Six we come to see that almsgiving is yes, giving coins, but more than that of giving up my "me" and my egocentric ways in favor of spiritual generosity with God at the center. Spiritual generosity leads us to spiritual liberation.

All of the instructions for examination of consciousness are intended for personal use at home in one's own time. The exercises are repeatable. On repetitions, the format does not change; however each one of us does. In repeating the exercises, especially in reviewing notes and circle meditations from previous examinations, the arc of one's spiritual growth can be seen.

The format is also suitable for group use: see "Small Group Formation Guidelines" found in Section Four. The group can meet weekly for one hour of contemplative prayer. At the close of the hour, weekly examination instructions can be given for individual/ at home use. A group prayer list of first names can be given to each participant, with the commitment to pray for one another daily for the course of the examination process. With respect to the integrity of the examination process, each one's spiritual journey is sacred onto oneself; however a group sharing experience can be arranged at the close of Week Six, for those who express an interest.

At the close of the examination period, in forming a faith commitment response, one may ask:

- What does spiritual liberation mean to me?
- What does spiritual generosity mean to me?
- How is my life so defined?

God has given us a fairly level playing field, with a wonderfully empty canvass, and loves us all unspeakably much. The examination period can be an enriching and artistic journey for the soul. Everyone has a story. Everybody brings something special. Each of us is the empty canvas, and God is the Artist in residence, painting the story of our lives on our hearts. God can do a most wondrous work in us when the canvas of our life is held empty and still.

There are artistic moments in each of us when the sacred and the obvious become one, and we are reminded that I am neither behind nor ahead: I am where I can be, sustained by God's grace.

FOR YOUR DAILY PRAYER

God's grace is experienced in many times and ways, and particularly in prayer. Our prayer is grounded in the word of God made known to us in reading the sacred scriptures. The effect of God's grace is to bring us back to our original and intended course, with a yearning for increased holiness and infinite goodness. It is our experience of God's grace that can then be reflected back to all of life. Follow the Lectio Divina instructions (next page) daily for the weeks of this examination period.

- Read daily for all six weeks: Matthew 11:28-30

In addition to Matthew 11:28, read daily the designated text for the week:

- Week One: Gratitude
  Psalm 91 "Under his wings … take refuge"
- Week Two: Examine
  John 12:23-26 "Unless a grain of wheat falls …"
- Week Three: Humility
  Philippians 4:8-13 "I can do all things through Christ …"
- Week Four: Forgiveness
  Isaiah 58:6-12 "… Repairer of the Breach"
- Week Five: Commitment
  Luke 9:18-27 "Follow me"
- Week Six: Gratitude
  2 Corinthians 5:17 "… a new creation."

READING THE SACRED SCRIPTURE: *LECTIO DIVINA*

The early Christians received the word of God face to face; what the apostles learned from Jesus they handed on to others orally. Prayer for the early Christians became repetitions of what was heard and remembered. Today every Christian is able to pick up a bible, hold it in their hands, and read the written word of God. The written word remains central to our faith when it is taken to heart and applied to one's life.

Lectio Divina, which translates to reading the divine word, is based on the premise that prayer must be rooted in the sacred scriptures, grounded in the word of God. The process of *Lectio Divina* suggests ways to evolve at one's own pace to a deeper understanding of the word of God. The practice has expanded into greater use in recent years with the growth in desire and understanding of the contemplative dimension to Christian spirituality.

Lectio Divina consists of reading (lectio), meditating (meditatio) and praying vocally, either silently or spoken (oratio), resulting in contemplation (contemplatio). In choosing a scripture passage, a verse within a chapter is sufficient. When one feels drawn to a certain text, repeated readings can be beneficial. There is always more to be seen when the living word of God is applied over time to one's life. Along the way of prayer, the word of God is transferred visually from written word to thought, leading to insights into one's life, guiding one toward silence in the blessed assurance of God's presence.

Twenty minutes is recommended. Find a balanced body posture. Select a passage. Read it slowly in the narrative form. Notice what verse, phrase or word remains with you. Reread the passage. Apply what you notice to your life. At this level we begin to see the sacred text as an overlay to our life, evoking thoughts and feelings. Something quite specific to your life may emerge out of the text you just read. Since the living word of God is truth this is a chance for your heart to be touched by God's truth. Slowly read the text again. Repeat all steps tomorrow with the same passage. Stay with the same passage until you are finished; that time may vary from a few days to a few weeks or months. For the course of this examination period one week is suggested.

In repeated readings we move from one level of prayer to another. As we do we are transformed from the inside out. When this method of prayer is practiced faithfully we find that we are truly living the words from the sacred scriptures, praying them from our heart out into our active life and feeling open to change: this is our ongoing conversion. We are being open and vulnerable to God at our deepest level. It is not particularly asking for anything more, but rather it is opening our hearts to be changed by God's grace. At the close of the third reading one may pray: "Lord, this is my life." Or "Lord, let this be my life."

Week One: Gratitude

God has given us a fairly level playing field
with a wonderfully empty canvas and
loves us all unspeakably much

Reading Instructions

For all six weeks read daily: Matthew 11:28-30
And for Week One read daily: Psalm 91
Suggested essay: "The Simplest Expression," page 57
Pray silently.

Examination Instructions

Meditate on the circle in its fullness. Be observant of your life.
Take your time between each of the following steps:

- Notice what in your life falls within your circle of oneness and wholeness.
- What pleases you and brings you toward fulfillment? Where do you find balance, or even enrichment? Where is your creativity energized?
- Consider all of the people, places and things of your life: your history, the present, your attitudes, your attachments and behaviors, events, circumstances, relationships, hopes, dreams and plans, whatever comes to your mind.
- The first 3-4-5 things you notice may be sufficient, or you may include whatever comes.

You may want to draw a symbol or write a word to represent each person, place or thing that comes up in you. Take time to experience gratitude for the aspects of your life that fall within the circle of oneness. Express your gratitude to God.

Practice this meditation daily, in order to deepen your awareness of what your life in God's grace is about at this time. Notice if there are any changes during the course of the week or if you find constancy. Every day is a new day.

WEEK TWO: EXAMINE

We stay faithful to our course
because we cannot do otherwise even in the face of
estrangement, rejection or reproval

Reading Instructions

For all six weeks read daily: Matthew 11:28-30
And for Week Two read daily: John 12:23-26
Suggested essay: "For it is in dying …" page 53
Pray silently.

Examination Instructions

Be observant of your life. Take your time between each step. Continue to follow the instructions from Week One, *and*:

Meditate on the circle in its fullness, and in its emptiness.

- Begin to notice what falls outside your circle of oneness and wholeness. What, or who in your life seems to cause disintegration? What, or who seems to pull you away from centeredness and a sense of wholeness?
- Consider all of the people, places and things of your life: your history, the present, your past, your attitudes, your attachments and behaviors, events, circumstances, relationships, events in your life, disappointments and matters that may feel unresolved, and places where you may feel blocked.
- The first 3-4-5 things you notice may be sufficient, or you may include whatever comes.

Take time to experience gratitude for the aspects of your life that fall within the circle of oneness and wholeness. This exercise asks that you be observant. There is no need to attend to solving or resolving anything. Practice this meditation daily, in order to deepen your awareness of what your life is all about at this time. See if there may be some clues here for your journey of examination of consciousness.

Express your gratitude to God for all that falls within the circle.

Week Three: Humility

> Everybody brings something special.
> If I cannot see this then I need to be a
> better observer and a better listener.

Reading Instructions

For all six weeks read daily: Matthew 11:28-30
And for Week Three read daily: Philippians 4:8-13
Suggested essay: "Courtesy of Heart" page 73
Pray silently.

Examination Instructions

Continue all steps from Weeks One and Two, *and*:
With the people, places and things that fall *outside* the circle of wholeness, meditate on them, and notice if there is anything:

- to be released, anything to let go of, perhaps because it's time?
- is it the weaker one who lets go? Or,
- is it the stronger one who lets go

Is there anything that could be brought into reconciliation by working with it, seeking a better understanding, praying for deeper insight, extending forgiveness, practicing humility, growing in faith? Are there specific points where humility could carry things forward? If not, can you identify one specific block?

Continue to be observant of your life. There is no need to move toward actively resolving anything. Learn to be observant of your life and the behavior of others.

Continue to express your gratitude to God for all that falls within the circle of oneness and wholeness. Has anything changed from Week One? Every day is a new day.

Focus on Humility

Humility is a pathway to forgiveness and spiritual liberation. In affirmation and reverence, out of humility I am careful to not make judgments or draw conclusions about another's behavior without information. Humility is:

- one's honest self-understanding liberated from self-absorption.
- living life without any mixture of motive.
- being able to speak without motive, no more and no less than is needed.
- a willingness to say: I believe I may be wrong, let me listen to you.
- remaining open to new insights about self and others.
- respecting the space between two people as the space wherein the Holy Spirit may live and move and breathe.
- a bend in the knee toward all of creation.

In my bending to another, I become open to the fact that I may be granted the grace to see what needs to be seen in me.

The Jesus Prayer: "Pray without ceasing" (1 Thessalonians 5:17)

The actual words of our prayer can be very brief. Our Christian faith is based on the life, death and resurrection of Jesus. Our prayer life is strengthened by the invocation of the name of Jesus;

the simple recitation of his name is a form of prayer. The name of Jesus can be used on its own, or inserted in a short or a long phrase, and repeated at length in slow intervals, with spaces between each repetition:

"Lord Jesus Christ, Son of God, have mercy on me."
"Jesus have mercy on me."
"Jesus have mercy."
"Jesus, mercy"
"Jesus."

Life is filled with waiting spaces. You can repeat the name of Jesus wherever you are: when sitting in your room or at your workplace, or when walking, or driving your car or wherever you happen to be. As well as using the name of Jesus freely it is also suggested that set times and places be established for the prayer, perhaps every morning on arising or at bedtime.

The body's posture should be one of physical balance and stability. Before you start saying the name of Jesus gather your awareness into your heart and pray to the Holy Spirit for inspiration. Do not *think* that you are invoking the name of Jesus. Simply repeat the name slowly, gently and calmly. Do not think of tangible results or outcomes. Leave space between each repetition; it is in the empty spaces in life where the Holy Spirit can live and move and breathe.

In our prayer, we are simply waiting on the name of Jesus. In our waiting we are granted the blessed assurance of God's grace: nothing more, and nothing less. Be willing to come to God empty handed and open hearted because "the Lord gives his blessing there, where he found the vessels empty" (Thomas à Kempis, *The Imitation of Christ* Bk IV, Ch. 15).

Your prayer becomes your own prayer of your heart. Other short repetitive prayers:

"Jesus, remember me when you come into your kingdom."
"O Lord, come to my assistance; make haste to help me."
"Thank you for the lessons learned today."
"O Lord, I am willing to wait on this."
"Change my heart, O God."
"Jesus, I trust in you"
"Jesus, mercy"

For the origins of the Jesus prayer: *The Way of a Pilgrim*, (Seabury Press) written in the 19th century by an anonymous Russian pilgrim monk.

WEEK FOUR: FORGIVENESS

God's grace is a felt sense in my body
Forgiveness is my search for a felt sense of God's grace
God's grace once given is for keeps

Reading Instructions

For all six weeks read daily: Matthew 11:28-30
And for Week Four read daily: Isaiah 58:6-12
Suggested essay: "For it is in giving ..." page 52
Pray silently.

Examination Instructions

Continue with all steps from previous weeks, *and*:

- consider what falls outside the circle of oneness and wholeness.
- notice if there is a particular *felt body sense* that comes with any of the people, places and things that fall outside the circle of oneness and wholeness.

Is there something that could be brought into reconciliation by seeking better understanding, praying for deeper insight, practicing humility, forgiveness, letting go (because it's time?) and seeking the realization that in all things, God is at work?

Be observant of your felt sense.

Focus on Forgiveness

- Is this a time to forgive someone?
- Is this a time to ask forgiveness of someone?
- Is this a time to forgive myself for something from the past?
- Is there a place for humility?
- What about this takes me sideways?
- What about this takes me backwards?
- What is a repairer of the breach? (Isaiah 58:12)
- Can the breach within you be repaired?
- Can the breach between you and another be repaired?
- What does spiritual liberation mean to me?
- What does spiritual generosity mean to me?
- Is there a point where there is release and rest from tension?
- What is *one small step* that could be taken to move forward?

Continue to express your gratitude to God for all that falls within your circle of oneness and wholeness.

Forgiveness in Relationships

Focus on one issue, the other person and yourself. Keep your responses brief; sometimes fewer words bring us closer to the truth.

- Describe the issue in concrete terms.
- Describe the other person.
- Recall times you have seen this person in a different way.
- Describe your inner turmoil over the unresolved issue.
- How does your inner turmoil act as a block to your creativity?

- What is one key to spiritual liberation?
- What is *one small step* that can be taken toward resolution of this issue?

Forgiveness bears witness in our world that love is stronger than wrong, and completes the mission of Jesus in our hearts.

WEEK FIVE: COMMITMENT

Nothing draws us quite so
powerfully as love
Where I am loved I'll go

Reading Instructions:

For all six weeks read daily: Matthew 11:28-30
And for Week Five read daily: Luke 9:23-27
Suggested essay: "Preferring Christ" page 67
Pray silently.

Examination Instructions

God uses points on earth to speak to us of heaven, and the orderliness of heaven cannot be disturbed. Meditate on all aspects of your life, and consider especially all that falls within the circle of oneness and wholeness. Drawn by love and grace, where I am loved, I will go: Jesus says, "Follow me."

- What is God calling me from, asking me to give up, or to let go?
- What is God calling me to in relationship to others, in my work, and in my behavior?
- What is the one thing holding me back?
- What is the one thing drawing me forward?
- How have I experienced God's blessing in the past from following God's call? How have I been blessed through

others who have followed God's call? How have others been blessed by my following God's call?

Jesus came to bear witness to all that is peaceful and good, the good that is the love of God. Jesus came to teach us the way we should go, the way of goodness. Jesus did not only come to teach goodness to the good; Jesus came to teach the one who would pause in life to listen.

"If anyone desires to come after Me,

Every journey has three parts to it
The part where I was
the part where I am and
the part where I will be
I can only be in one place at a time

Let him deny himself

My false self lives through the people, places and things around me
in truth, I am God's

And take up his cross daily

I cannot take up his cross
If my hands are filled
With too many people, places and things
From the past, the present or I have worries about the future

And follow Me."

Luke 9:23

Week Six: Gratitude

The contemplative heart towers above nothing
embraces all, loves God, loves neighbor and
forgives all the rest

Reading Instructions

For all six weeks read daily: Matthew 11:28-30
And for Week Six read daily: 2 Corinthians 5:17
Suggested essay: "The Contemplative Heart" page 92
Pray silently.

Examination Instructions

Contemplative observation implies the ability to watch and
wait: to look at and reflect on what we see with feeling as well as
thought, and with involvement as well as detachment. Ultimately
the choice remains ours. We do not seek to be perfect, but we do
seek the refining influence of God's grace.

Take your time between each of the following steps:

- Meditate on the circle in its fullness.
- Be observant of your life.
- Notice what in your life falls within the circle of oneness
  and wholeness.
- What pleases you and brings you toward fulfillment?
  Where do you find balance, or even enrichment? Where
  is your creativity energized?
- How do I define spiritual generosity?
- What does spiritual liberation mean to me?
- How is my way of life so defined?

Express your gratitude to God.

Everything in the spiritual life is preparation for what is to
come. If we were asked to go on alone, we would fail. Through
prayer in the body of Christ, we are granted the grace to touch the

ground that is holy and stable, the ground of God. This is the place where reconciliation of all things stands as mystical fact, and our invitation to be there is unceasing.

> *So if anyone is in Christ, there is a new creation!*
> — 2 Corinthians 5:17

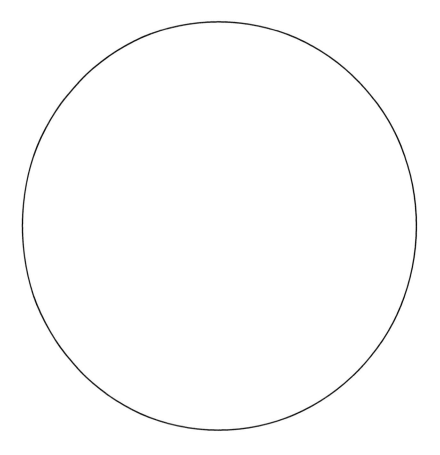

Section Four: Small Group Formation Guidelines

*"For where two or three are gathered in my name,
I am there among them."* – Matthew 18:20

Small Group Formation Guidelines

The following guidelines are offered to provide practical support for parish faith formation programs. The guidelines are also useful for establishing a disciplined prayer practice for use at home in one's own time. While one can read through any of the guidelines given for the practice of contemplative prayer, being able to pray with a group on a regular basis is the better-known source of encouragement for one's individual spiritual development.

The group model shows a group meeting once a week. The facilitator may choose to establish a group that meets weekly, bi-monthly or once a month. Another option is to select a set of essays from "Section Two: Brief Spiritual Essays" and meet for that number of weeks. For example: the unit on The Lord's Prayer contains eight essays, and would be suitable for eight consecutive prayer meetings. Alternatively, one set of essays may be used to form the focus for a weekend retreat.

The format given is for one-hour meetings. A disciplined one-hour commitment is easier to keep on a regular basis, as opposed to one that is predictably longer or open-ended. The hour has no spare parts to take away from our common purpose. One hour is the time frame given by Jesus:

"Could you not stay awake with me one hour?"
– Matthew 26:40

Contemplative Prayer Group Model:

"Come to me, all you that are weary,
and I will give you rest."
– Matthew 11:28

Every Tuesday evening   7:30 to 8:30
7:30 quiet gathering and transition time
7:35 brief reading
7:40 silent prayer
8:00 walking meditation (optional)
8:05 silent prayer
8:25 we pray together: *"Our Father … "*

Closing prayer, we pray together:

Keep us Lord as we wake,
guard us as we sleep,
that awake we may keep with Christ,
and asleep rest in his peace.

Some prefer to keep the silence and depart at this time. If you wish, please stay for a few minutes of conversation regarding the reading and the practice of contemplative prayer.

We are a (Catholic/Lutheran/Methodist etc.) Christian community. Realizing we are all more alike than we are different, we welcome those of other faith traditions, as well as those exploring their spirituality. Please join us once, often or always, for the Love of it!

For further information, please contact: (facilitator name/contact information)

Where there is no love, put love, and you will draw out love.
    – St. John of the Cross, *The Minor Words*

WHY DO WE DO WHAT WE DO?

7:30-7:35   quiet gathering and transition time

When we come in the door, we leave behind us all the people, places and things of our active/outer life, insofar as we are able. We will get back to all of it soon enough, but for now each one of us moves toward finding some sense of oneness within oneself. This transition step is often skipped within the context of our daily life. We are more inclined to go directly from arrival to purpose. Here we take three steps: 1) time to arrive 2) time to acquire a sense of presence and 3) time to become aware of our common purpose.

7:35   brief reading (one essay selected from Section Two)

The reading serves to bring us to one body, offers some words of insightful instruction regarding our spiritual journey, and points us in the direction of openness to God in prayer. Thoughts gathered from the reading are not necessarily taken with us into the prayer times. The reading may generate brief discussion after the close of prayer, and form a focus for prayer in the week to come.

7:40-8:00   first period silent prayer

Contemplative prayer is our simple and silent surrender to our God who loves us. It is as if we say "Lord I am here for you, and I know that you are here for me too." Or "Change my heart O God." We desire to be the empty canvas; God is the artist. During prayer, thoughts will come and go. We do not eliminate thoughts from our mind; that would be an impossible task that would only take us sideways. We neither accept nor reject the thoughts that come; we merely acknowledge the interruptive nature of our restless mind. When the inevitable thoughts do come, it may be helpful to use a simple word or phrase to bring your focus back to God; that is to return to conscious contact with the ground, the ground of God.

For most of us, our lives consist of unrelenting input. Silent prayer is an opportunity for God to perhaps "get a word in edgewise" into our busy lives and have an effect on us. We experience moments of God's grace. God's grace is for keeps, is cumulative in us, and brings us to change. We call the change transformation, or conversion. Because transformation in this way comes slowly, we very gradually over time begin to see that the changes within become effective and permanent components of our spiritual nature.

8:00 to 8:05   walking meditation – optional

The walking meditation is done very slowly, around the perimeter of the chapel or prayer space, following one another with spaces in between. This serves as a break in the prayer, shows us that we can take prayer to our active/outer/moving life, and reminds us that with many things in life, we can slow down from time to time and it will be ok. In the walking meditation, we have high regard for the spaces between persons, as this is the space wherein the Holy Spirit can live and move and breathe.

8:05-8:25 second period silent prayer

8:25 closing prayer   We pray together "The Lord's Prayer" and "Keep us Lord as we wake."

WHY DO WE DO THE MEDITATION WALK?

In very simple and practical terms, the meditation walk gives us a break between the two prayer periods. Untrained human nature cannot sustain focused attention for one hour. We can manage 20 minutes. For example, if you think about a wait in a doctor's office, 10-15-20 minutes feels within the limits of our expectations. If you wait for anyone or anything for over 25 or 30 minutes, one may begin to feel restless, annoyed and distracted. We stay within what feels manageable. After the walking meditation, we become refocused for the second period of prayer. Perhaps we begin from a different place than at the outset.

In the walking meditation we feel high regard for the space between us and the person behind and the person in front of us.

The spaciousness between two or more of us is where the Spirit lives and moves and breathes. The space is to be valued. Can I give myself the space that is needed in order for me to fully function in my life? Can I give the same to others?

In the walking meditation we seek our ground, the holy ground of God given to us this day. We remain grounded in this way: foot forward, landing on heel, slowly moving forward to the ball of the foot. When the foot in front is firmly grounded, then the rear foot lifts to leave to move forward in the same way, landing on heel, rolling to the ball of the foot, becoming firmly grounded as it receives the weight of the body. In this way we always remain in conscious contact with the ground, the ground of our prayer.

The walking meditation is done very slowly. Questions we may ask: What on earth would happen if I were to slow down, pull back a little in my life? Is faster really better? Or is less really more? As I walk what am I asked to leave behind? What is God calling me from? What is God calling me to?

> *I was overjoyed to find some of your children walking in the*
> *truth, just as we have been commanded by the Father.*
> *– 2 John 1:4*

Some practical instructions, for one who feels drawn to practice contemplative prayer:

1. Find a posture that gives you a balanced feeling in your body.
   Sitting with body weight balanced and with a straight back facilitates easier and deeper breathing. Breathing may become slowed, as well as deeper, as the outer things of life are released.

> *Be submissive as is the statue to the craftsman who molds it,*
> *to the artist who paints it, and to the gilder who embellishes it.*
> *– St. John of the Cross, The Minor Works*

2. Set aside all that you carry with you in your heart and hands.

We come to God empty-handed and open-hearted insofar as we are able, trusting that God knows all of our needs and will care for us. Set aside, just for now all the people, places and things of your active/outer life. Set aside also reading materials and other meditation objects (may be placed on the counter in the outer room). Take a moment to experience what it is like to entrust your whole sense of being completely to God, and prepare to receive God's presence and action within. Be the empty canvass, and allow God to be the artist. We know that through Jesus, by the power of the Holy Spirit, God is brought closer to us than our own thinking and even closer than touch.

For the Lord gives his blessing there, where he found the vessels empty.
– Thomas à Kempis, *The Imitation of Christ,* Book IV, Chapter 15

3.   Choose a sacred word or phrase that feels special to you.

During the prayer, sounds come in from outside, and thoughts come up from within. When we become aware of these distractions, it can be helpful to have a simple and sacred word to repeat silently within. For example: "Jesus" "Mercy" "Peace" or "Jesus have mercy on me." Inner and outer distractions are a normal part of the prayer process and there is no goal to eliminate them, but to gently notice a return to prayer by using a sacred word. We remain grounded in the process of prayer, and not attached to outcomes.

Trust in God's grace. God knows all of our needs. All is in God's hands. All is grace. It may be sufficient to pray: "Lord, take me back" or "Change my heart O Lord"

4.   Express your gratitude to God.

I have loved you with an everlasting love. – Jeremiah 31:3

The creative spirit soars
when given free reign
in the ground of God.

The following single essay is provided for the facilitator and the group to apply the guidelines to the actual small group formation process:

GOD'S MERCY: THE GRACE OF TENDERNESS

The Lord is my Shepherd, I shall not want. – Psalm 23:1

If at a distance we could witness the life of the shepherd with his flock, we might likely see what could be termed acts of contemplative tenderness. From that imagined vision, one might wonder how to cultivate a culture of tenderness. Tenderness is one of the things that could be felt most missing in our world today. How different life would be in a culture of tenderness where rituals, rules and routines would be modified and softened from what prevails today. We know that in truth there is another side to life, a quieter more reflective side to life that comes from the mysterious effects of remaining close to the protection of God's grace; a place where we know in fact that we are loved, and called precious in God's sight (Isaiah 43:4).

Jesus is our True Shepherd, the one who provides us with the consolations and explanations not found here on earth. In the universal unbroken bond of silence, in our prayer today we can feel touched by the grace of God's tenderness. By the touch of God's grace, we can feel relieved of the tensions of our divisions. The shepherd gives the sheep protection from harm; the shepherd will protect those who remain, and will seek out the one who strays.

The sheep do well to stay close to their master. So do we. Jesus has experienced our divisions and sorrows, and endured our struggles in life. It is our lifelong goal to model our behavior after Jesus. By the power and inspiration of the Holy Spirit, we are granted the grace to do so. In prayer, we may clearly renew our request to remain under God's guidance. In asking, I become more conscious of receiving. Having received, I know that the only measurement of my gratitude is the extent to which I am able to give to others what

God has given to me: the heartfelt knowledge of the tenderness and the protection of God's unending grace. It is here where I choose to remain, under the continual guidance of our Good Shepherd.

> *"I am the good shepherd. I know my own and my own know me, just as the Father knows me and I know the Father. And I lay down my life for the sheep."* – John 10:14-15

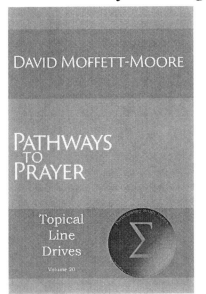

More from Energion Publications

Christian Living

Grief: Finding the Candle of Light	Jody Neufeld	$8.99
My Life Story	Becky Lynn Black	$14.99
Crossing the Street	Robert LaRochelle	$16.99
Tithing after the Cross	David Croteau	$9.99
Rendering Unto Caesar	Chris Surber	$5.99

Bible Study

From Inspiration to Understanding	Edward W. H. Vick	$24.99
When People Speak for God	Henry Neufeld	$17.99
Philippians: A Participatory Study Guide	Bruce Epperly	$9.99
Ephesians: A Participatory Study Guide	Robert D. Cornwall	$9.99
Meditations on According to John	Herold Weiss	$14.99

Theology

Creation in Scripture	Herold Weiss	$12.99
Creation: the Christian Doctrine	Edward W. H. Vick	$12.99
The Politics of Witness	Allan R. Bevere	$9.99
Ultimate Allegiance	Robert D. Cornwall	$9.99
The Journey to the Undiscovered Country	William Powell Tuck	$9.99
Process Theology	Bruce G. Epperly	$4.99

Spirituality

Holy Smoke! Unholy Fire	Bob McKibben	$14.99
Hunger	Jon Dybdahl	$12.99
Assenting to the Eternal	Carolyn Côté	$9.99
Holistic Spirituality	Bruce G. Epperly	$5.99
Process Spirituality (Forthcoming)	Bruce G. Epperly	$5.99
Pathways to Prayer	David Moffett-Moore	$5.99
Life as Pilgrimage	David Moffett-Moore	$14.99

Generous Quantity Discounts Available
Dealer Inquiries Welcome
Energion Publications — P.O. Box 841
Gonzalez, FL 32560
Website: http://energionpubs.com
Phone: (850) 525-3916